Port Perry Ontario in Colour Photos, Saving Our History One Photo at a Time

Photography
by Barbara Raué
©2022

Series Name: Cruising Ontario

Book 220: Port Perry

Cover photo: Corner of Water and Queen Streets, Page 39

©All the photos in this book have been taken with my cameras. I own the rights to them.

Series Name: Cruising Ontario
Saving Our History One Photo at a Time
in colour photos

Books Available in Alphabetical Order:
Aberfoyle, Acton, Ajax, Alton, Amherstburg, Ancaster, Arthur, Auburn, Aylmer, Ayr, Beaver Valley, Belgrave, Belleville, Bloomingdale, Blyth, Brantford, Brockville, Burford, Burlington, Caledon, Caledonia, Cambridge, Carlow, Chatsworth, Clifford, Collingwood, Conestogo, Delhi, Dorchester to Aylmer, Drayton, Drumbo, Dundas, Dunlop, Eden Mills, Elmira, Elora, Erin, Essex, Fergus, Goderich, Grimsby, Guelph, Hagersville, Hamilton, Hanover, Harriston, Hespeler, Jarvis, Kingston, Kingsville, Kitchener, Lake Superior, Lincoln, Linwood, Listowel, London, Lucknow, Merrickville, Mono, Mount Forest, Mount Pleasant, Neustadt, New Hamburg, Newboro, Newport, Niagara-on-the-Lake, Niagara Falls, North Bay, Oakville, Onondaga, Orangeville, Orillia, Oshawa, Owen Sound, Palmerston, Paris, Pelham, Perth, Peterborough, Petrolia, Pickering, Port Colborne, Port Elgin, Portland, Preston, Rockwood, Sarnia, Sault Ste. Marie, Seaforth, Sheffield, Shelburne, Simcoe, Smiths Falls, Smithville, Southampton, St. Catharines, St. George, St. Jacobs, St. Marys, St. Thomas, Stoney Creek, Stratford, Thamesford, Thunder Bay, Tillsonburg, Toronto, Waterdown, Waterford, Waterloo, Welland, Wellesley, West Flamborough, Westport, Whitby, Windsor, Wingham, Woodstock

Book 207-209: Niagara Falls
Book 210: North Bay
Book 211: Fort Erie
Book 212-215 Haldimand County
Book 216: Sudbury

Book 217: Parry Sound
Book 218-219: Uxbridge
Book 220: Port Perry

Table of Contents

Port Perry

Perry Street	Page 5
Queen Street	Page 15
Casimir Street	Page 36
Mary Street	Page 37
Bigelow Street	Page 40
North Street	Page 40
Water Street	Page 42
Epsom	Page 50

Port Perry is a community located in Scugog, Ontario. The town is located northeast of Toronto and just north of Oshawa. The area around Port Perry was first surveyed as part of Reach Township by Major S. Wilmot in 1809. The first settler in the area was Reuben Crandell, a United Empire Loyalist who built a homestead with his wife in May 1821.

Settler Peter Perry laid out village lots on the shore of Lake Scugog in 1848 on the site of a former native village known as Scugog Village. The town site was named Port Perry in 1852 and its first Postmaster was Joseph Bigelow.

The first train on the Port Whitby and Port Perry Railway reached the terminus in Port Perry in 1872. Cargo from all over northern Ontario was shipped via the Trent-Severn Waterway to Port Perry via Lake Scugog, and then via the railway to Whitby, where it could be loaded onto the Canadian Pacific or Canadian National mainlines running along the shore of Lake Ontario, or onto ships in Port Whitby.

The village was amalgamated with Cartwright, Reach and Scugog Townships to form the Township of Scugog in 1974 upon the creation of the Regional Municipality of Durham.

On July 3, 1884 the entire business section of Port Perry was destroyed by fire. The wooden buildings exploded when sparks hit them. The Ross & Sons Grain Elevator on the waterfront, plus two other buildings were the only ones to survive. Thirty-three commercial buildings housing nearly fifty businesses, as well as factories, warehouses, stables, six lodges, and a dozen homes were reduced to rubble in under an hour.

Four months later, the entire commercial sector with seventeen large brick buildings were built.

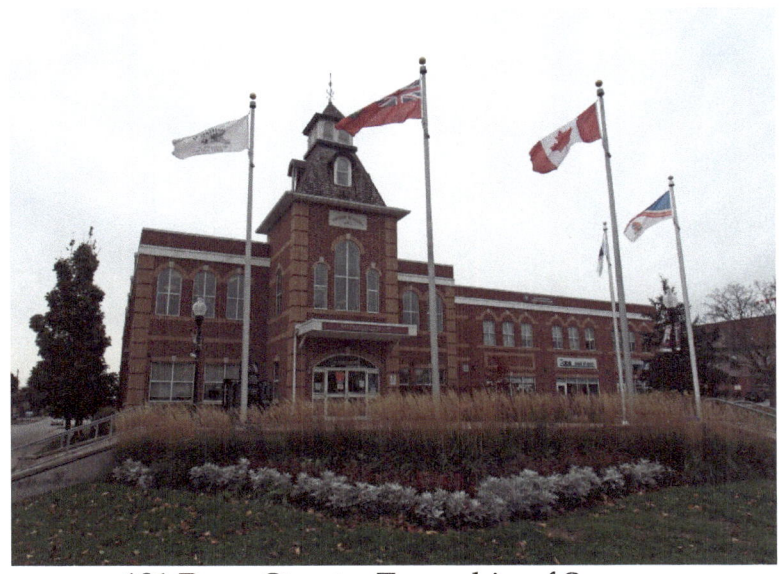

181 Perry Street – Township of Scugog

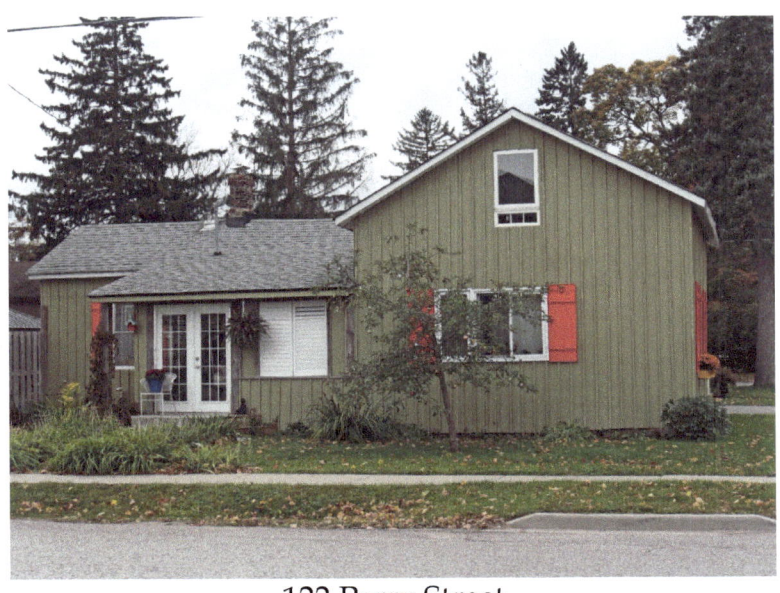

122 Perry Street

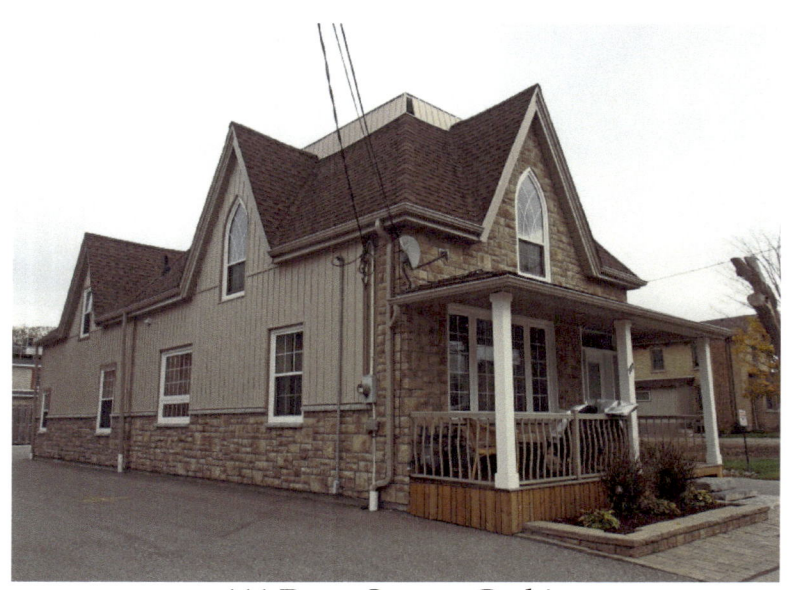

111 Perry Street - Gothic

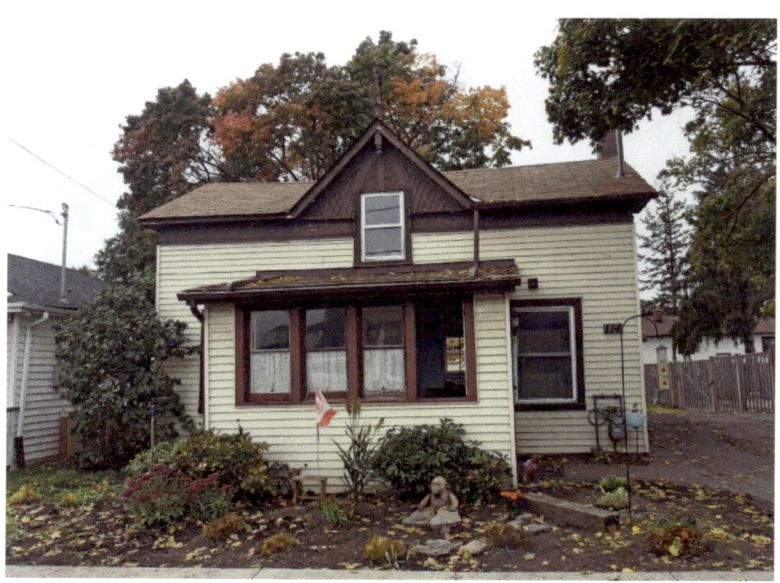

114 Perry Street

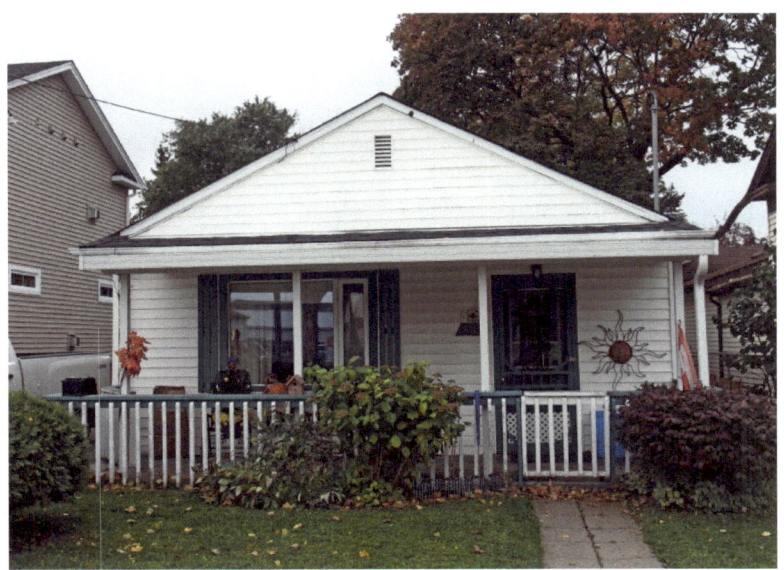

110 Perry Street

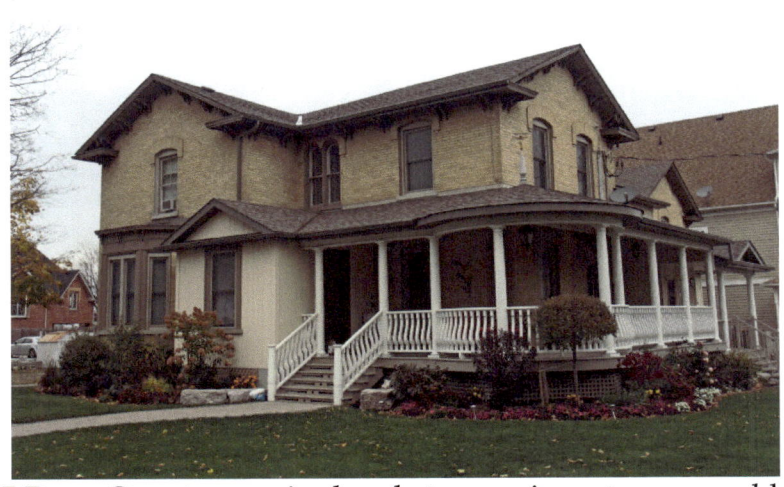

95 Perry Street – cornice brackets, cornice return on gables

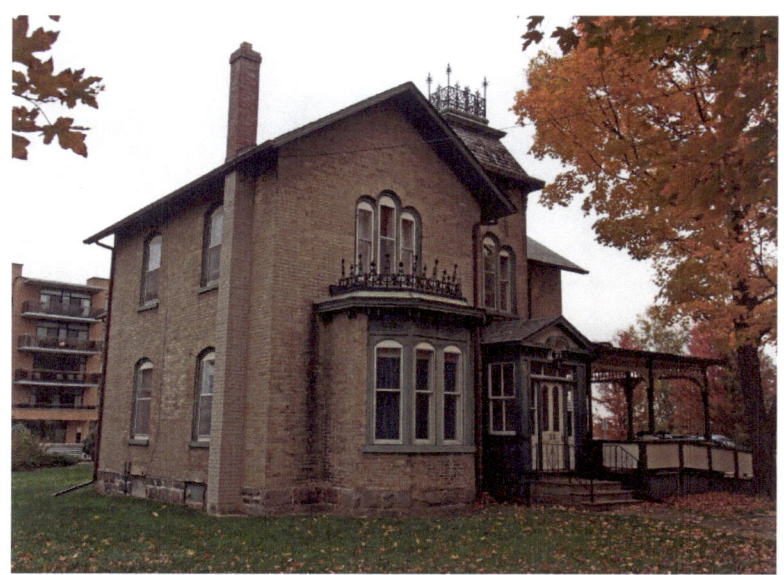

53 Perry Street - The Burnham House is a two story brick house that was built for John W. Burnham in 1878. The house is located on a large lot that overlooks Lake Scugog to the east. Mr. Burnham served as the local postmaster for 45 years.

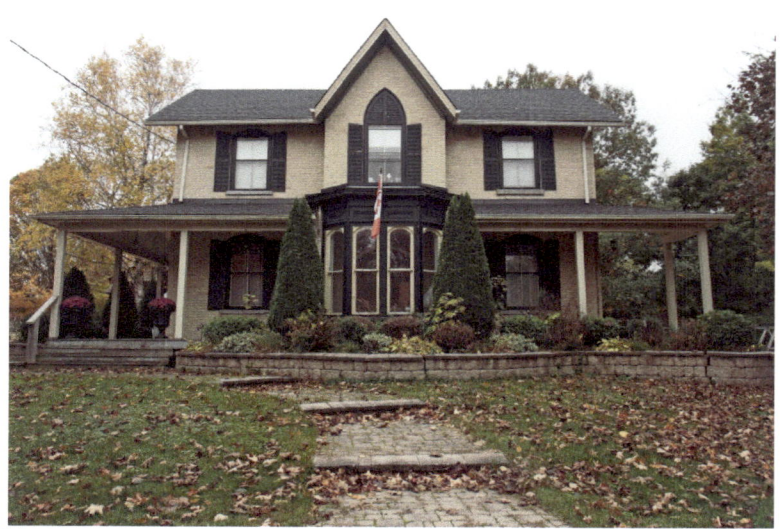

56 Perry Street – Campbell House - 2 story, brick, c. 1876

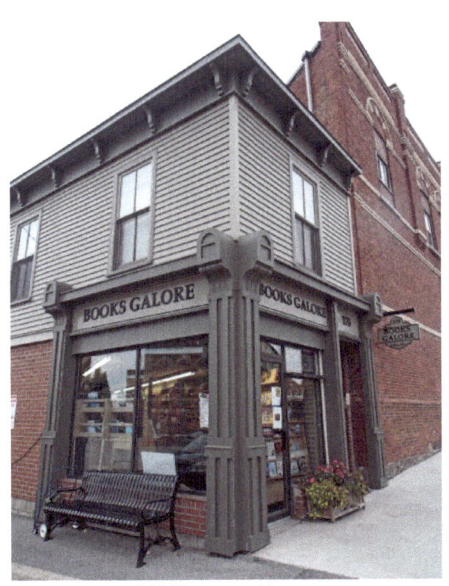

175 Perry Street

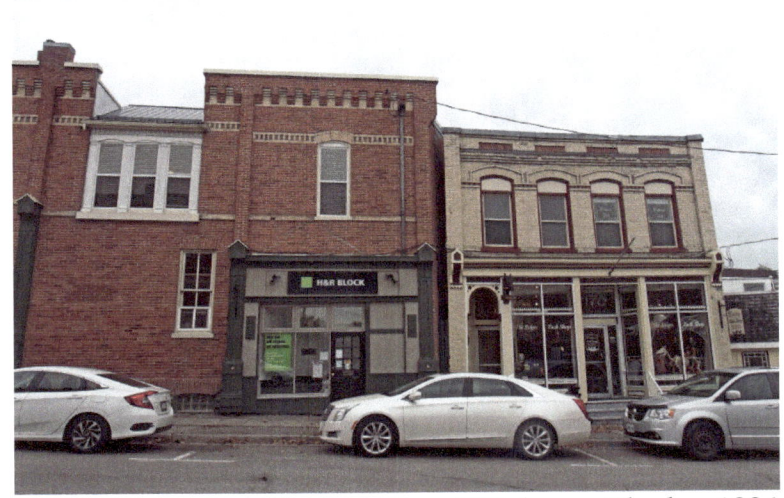

174-176 Perry Street - The Laing and Meharry Block – 1884 – The two easterly units of the original three section block are owned by the Brock family who occupy four storefronts.

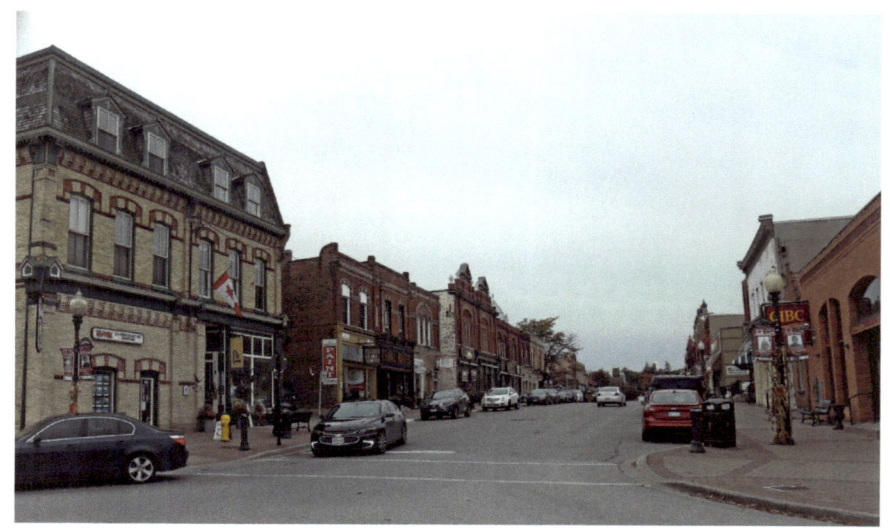

154 Queen Street – Construction of the Ackerman Block was completed in 1888. Benjamin F. Ackerman was a leading manufacturer of harness and many other leather products including trunks and saddles. The eastern half is now the Village Décor Shoppe (second building on the left side).

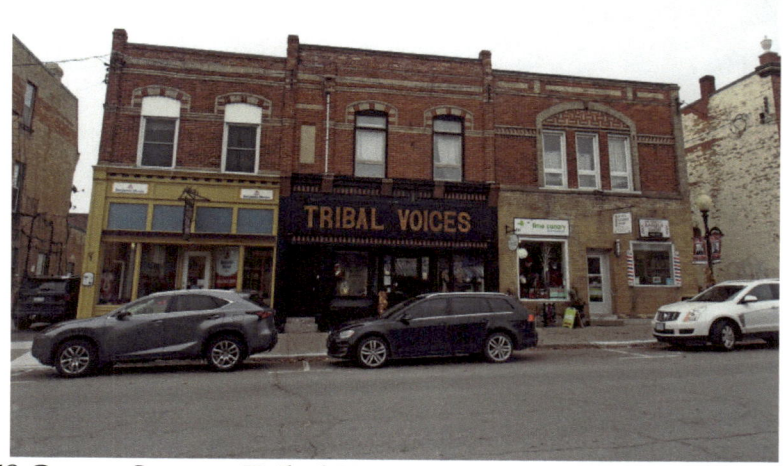

158 Queen Street – Tribal Voices Jewelry and Watches Store

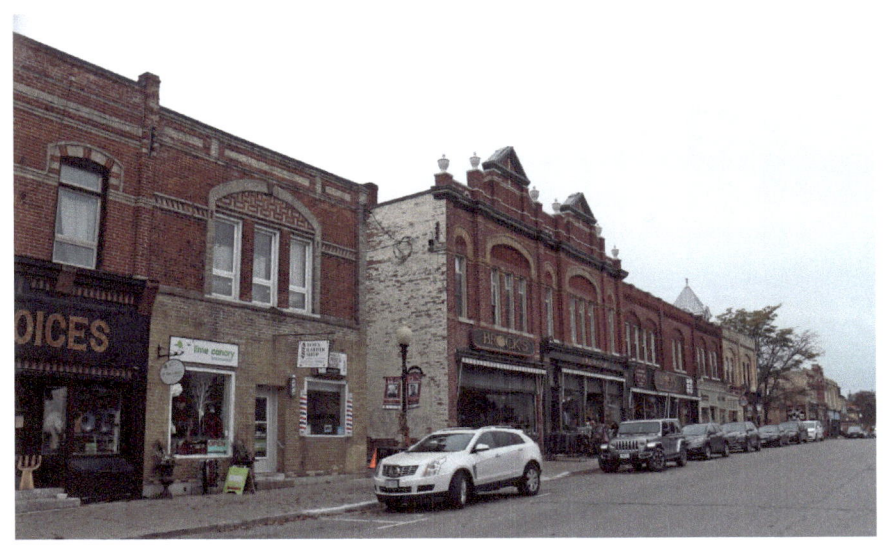

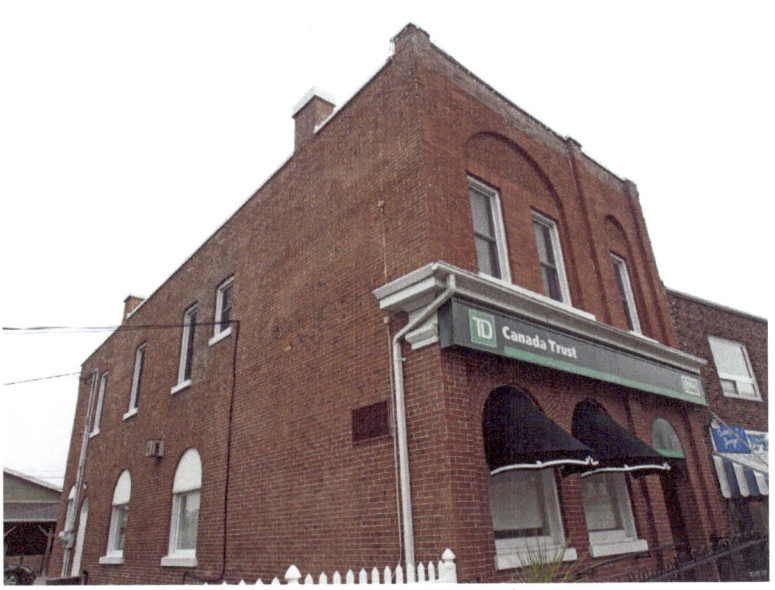

165 Queen Street – Canada Trust

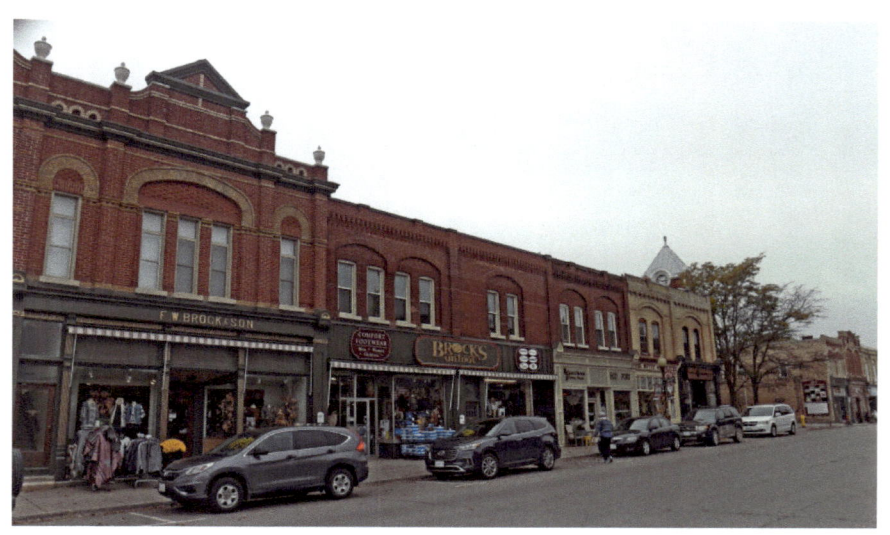

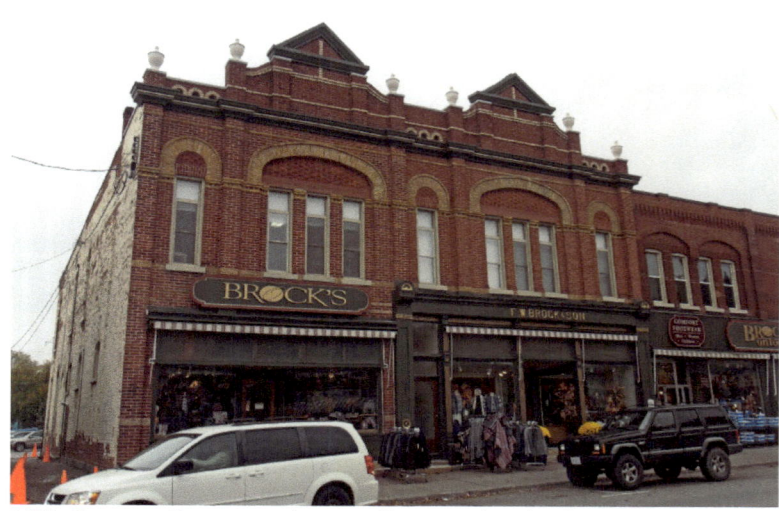

168-178 Queen Street – Aaron Ross rebuilt this two-story building in 1885 after being destroyed by fire. In 1911, Ross sold his business to William Brock who opened a general store. The building and business has been owned and operated by members of the Brock family for more than a century.

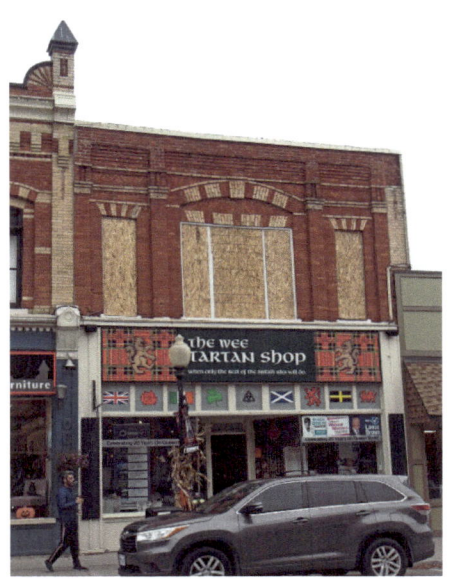

177 Queen Street – The Wee Tartan Shop

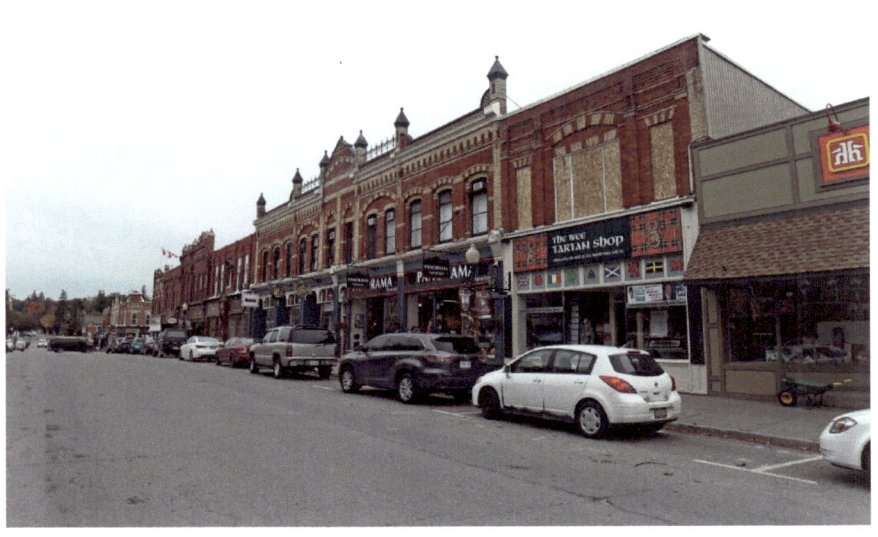

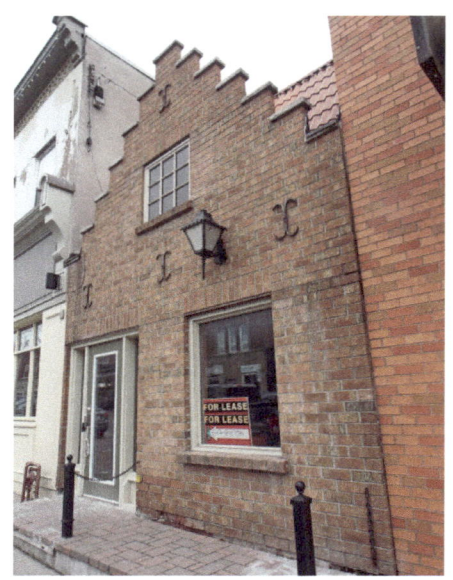
Queen Street – stepped parapet

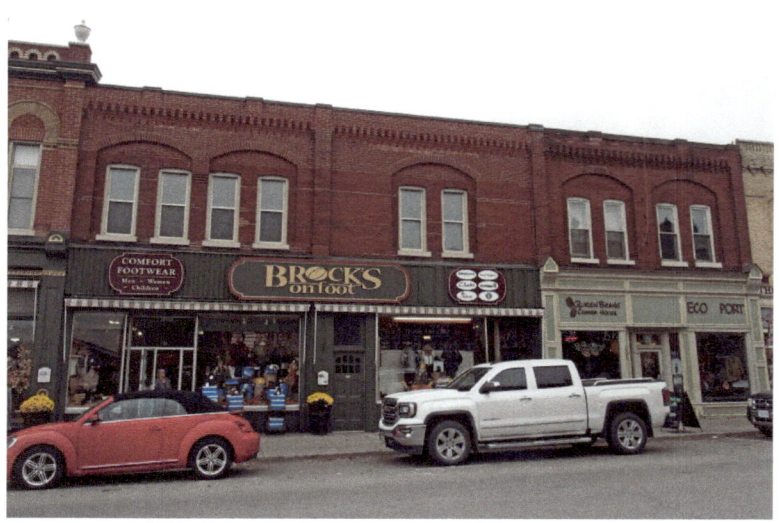
178 Queen Street – Brock's On Foot

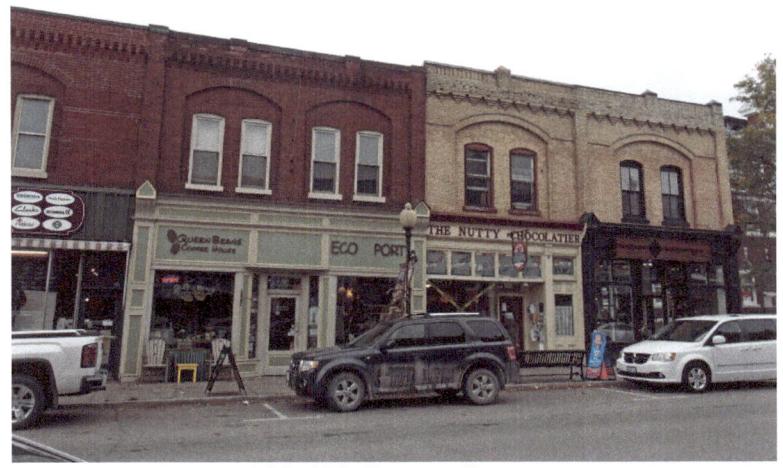

180-182 Queen Street

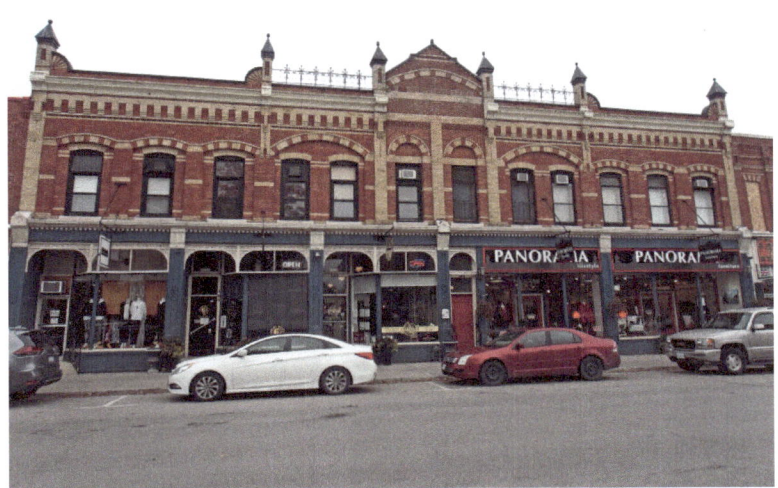

183-189 Queen Street – This impressive red and yellow brick building was constructed in 1885 by Jonathan Blong. He divided the building into a number of units which were leased to local shopkeepers.

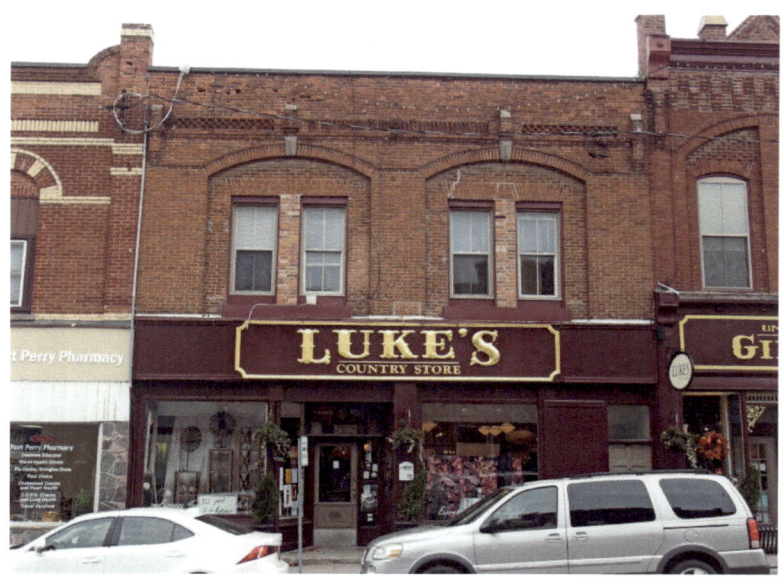

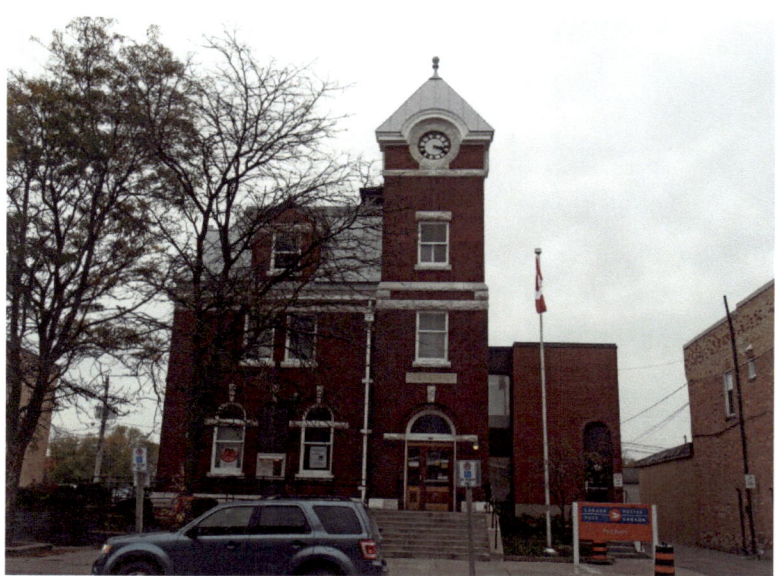

192 Queen Street – Post Office

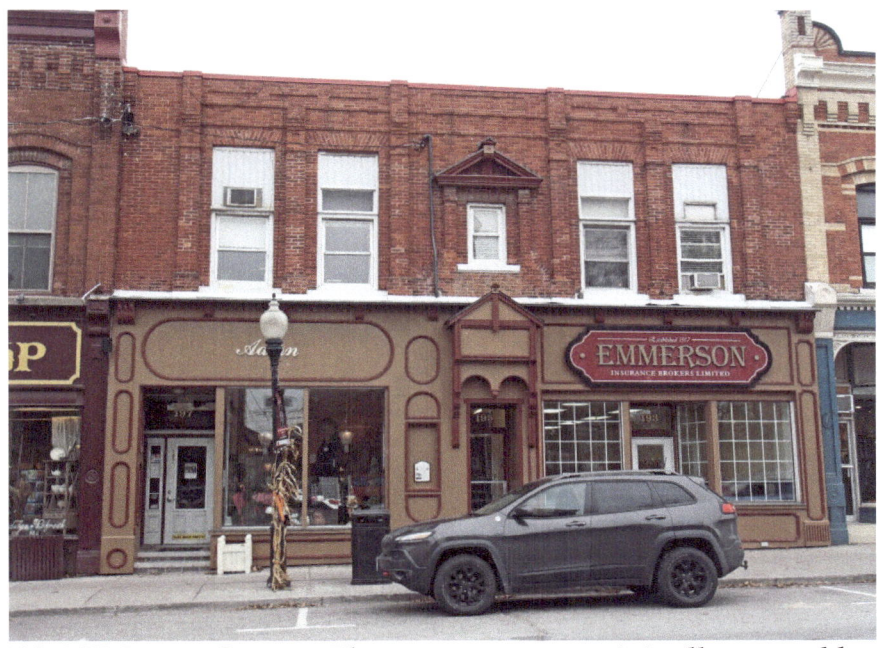

193-197 Queen Street – The property was originally owned by Port Perry entrepreneur Joseph Bigelow; after the fire he transferred the building to his son-in-law William Henry McCaw where he operated his jewellery store; he leased the western portion to local clothier William F. Brock. Emmerson Insurance has operated in Port Perry since 1917 and continues to operate from this location.

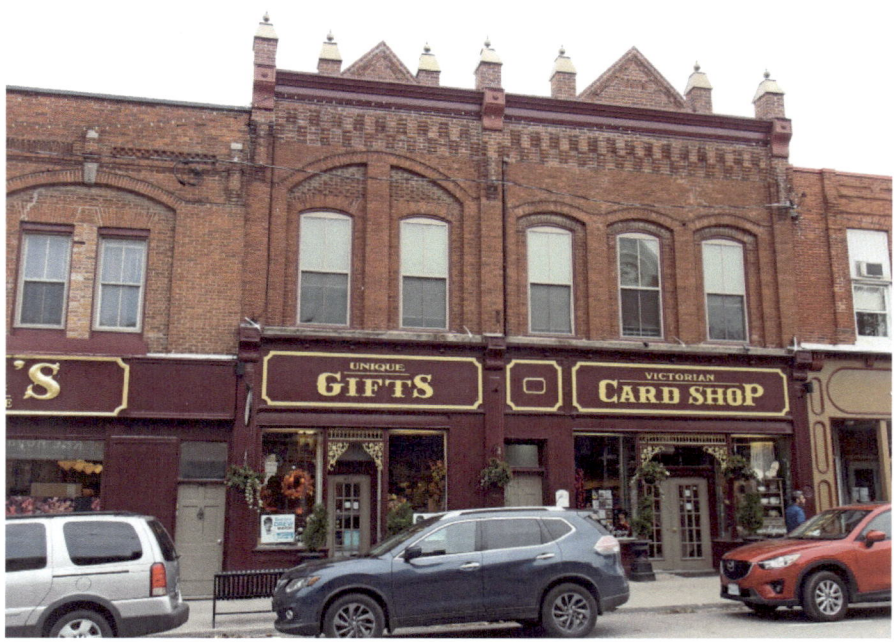

201-203 Queen Street – William Jones formed a partnership with John McClung when this new building was built after the fire destroyed the earlier building in 1884. Clothes, groceries, crockery, boots and shoes were sold. Charles Jones operated a dry goods store in the eastern part. In 1988 the property was purchased by Wayne and Carolyn Luke who opened the Victorian Card Shop in this section.

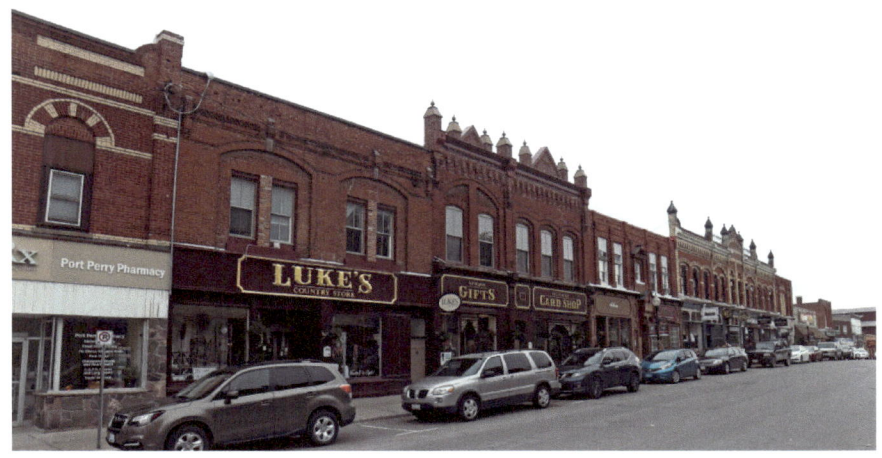

205-207 Queen Street - William L. Parrish Block – E. Worthington built a flour and feed store here in 1868. W. T. Parrish later bought it and turned it into a hardware store. Immediately after the July 1884 fire, Mr. Parrish turned over ownership to his 20-year-old son, W.L. Parrish, who built the present two-story brick building and reopened it in February 1886. The store continued under the Parrish name until he sold it to W. Harry Peel in 1946. When Mr. Peel went out of business, Wes Lane, a former employee, took over the plumbing side of the business and the building was divided into two separate stores. The eastern half was occupied by a ladies' clothing store named Canadian Women and later Yvonne's. In 1976 the building was sold to Wayne and Carolyn Luke. The Lukes later purchased the adjoining building to the east and made it into one unit again.

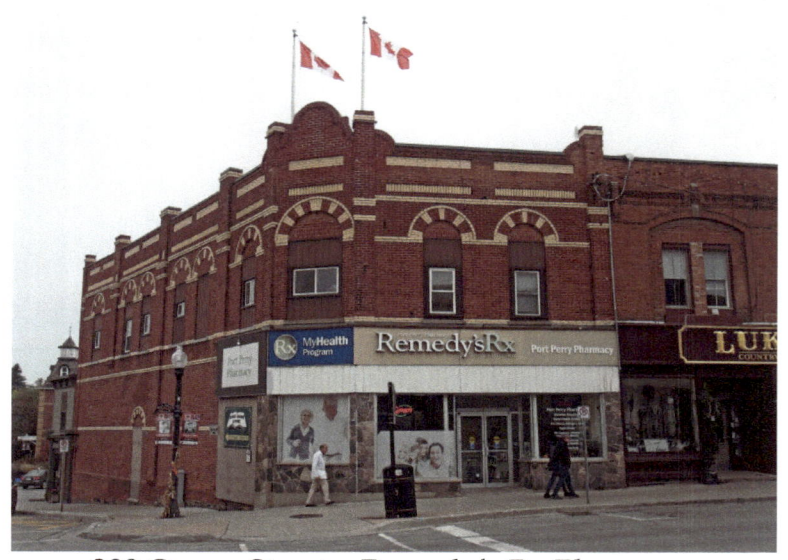

209 Queen Street – Remedy's Rx Pharmacy

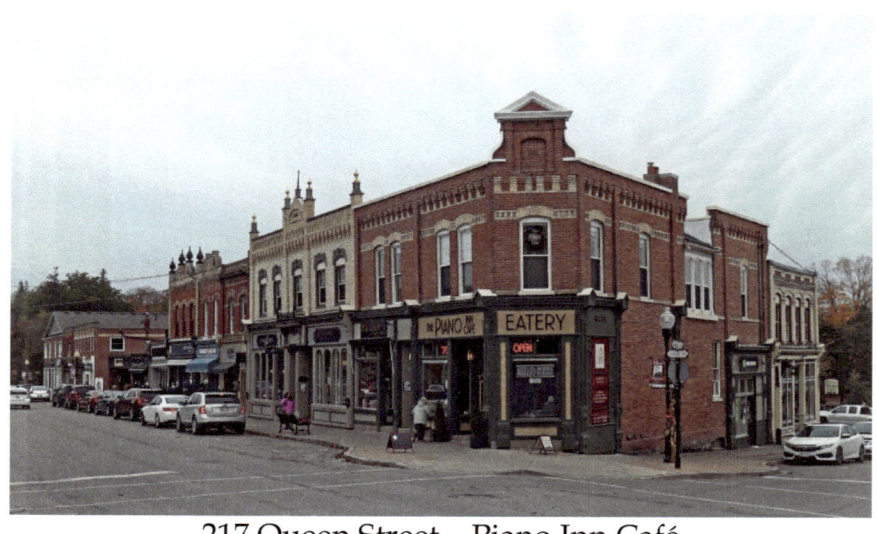

217 Queen Street – Piano Inn Café

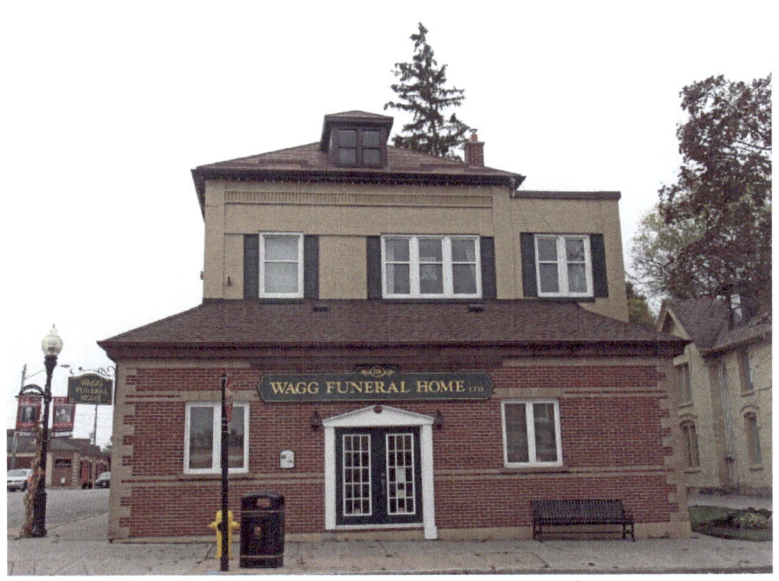

216 Queen Street – Wagg Funeral Home – John W. Davis opened a furniture manufacturing shop here in 1846; he also made coffins and acted as undertaker. The present building was built in 1884. Harold Wagg purchased it in 1981.

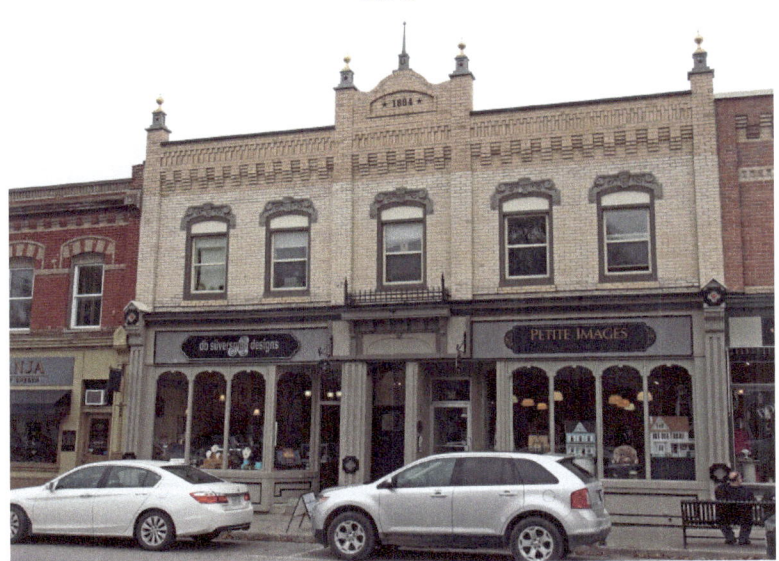

223-227 Queen Street - 1884

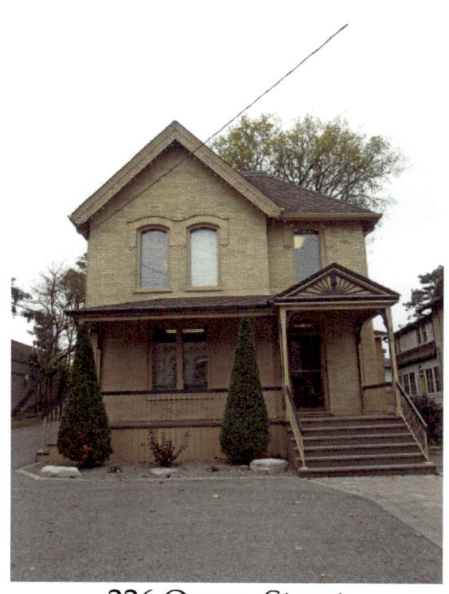

226 Queen Street

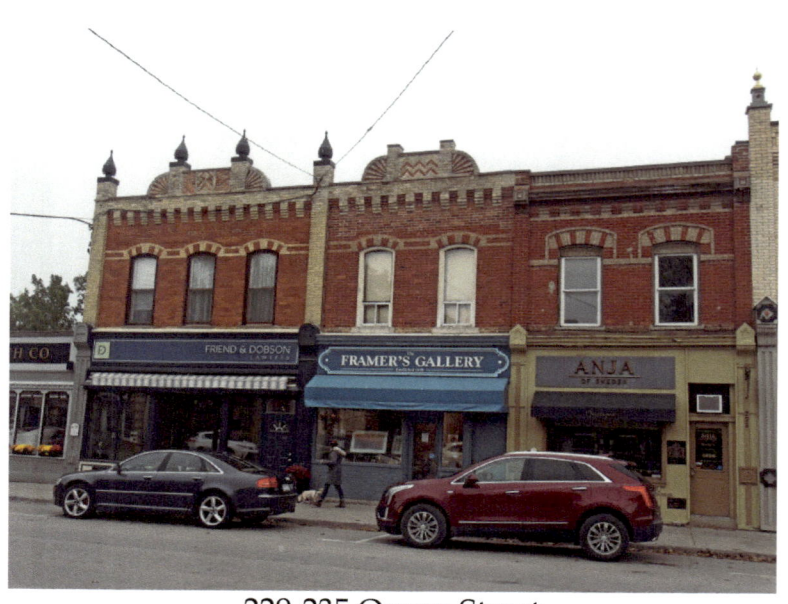

229-235 Queen Street

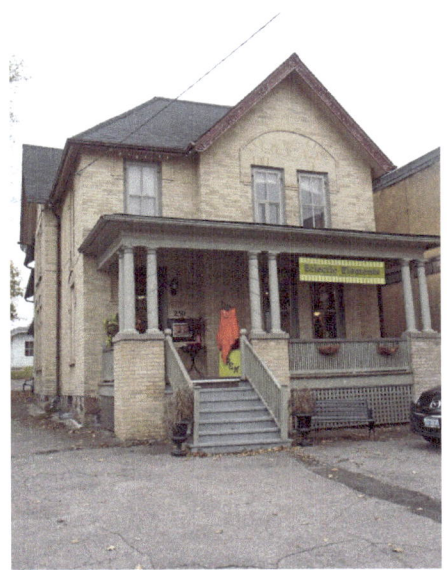

230 Queen Street

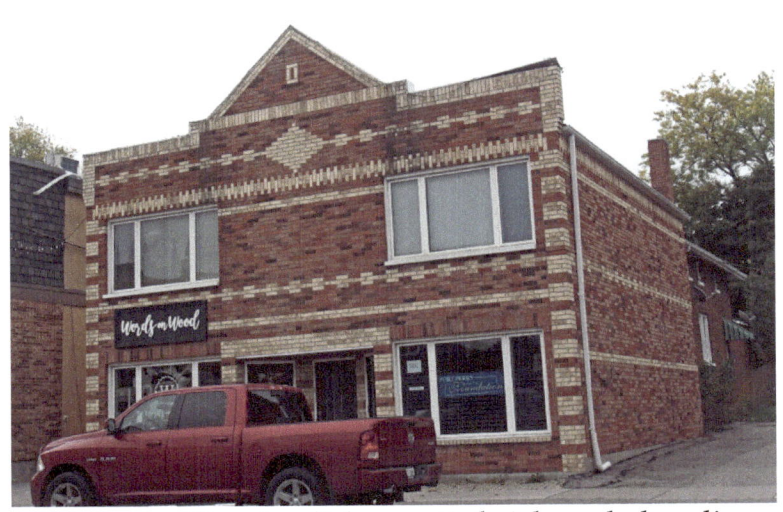

242 Queen Street – dichromatic brickwork, banding

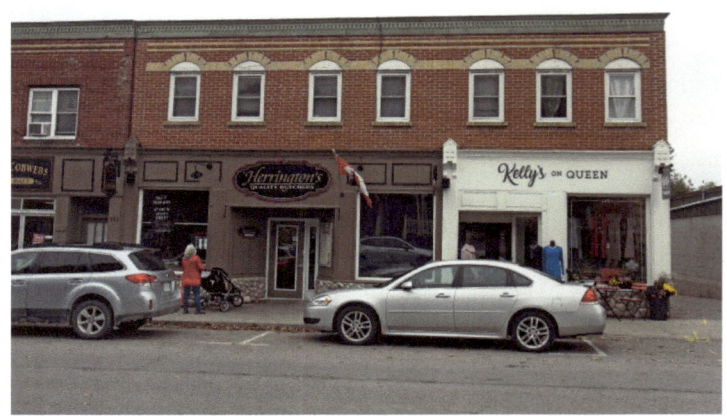

249-253 Queen Street

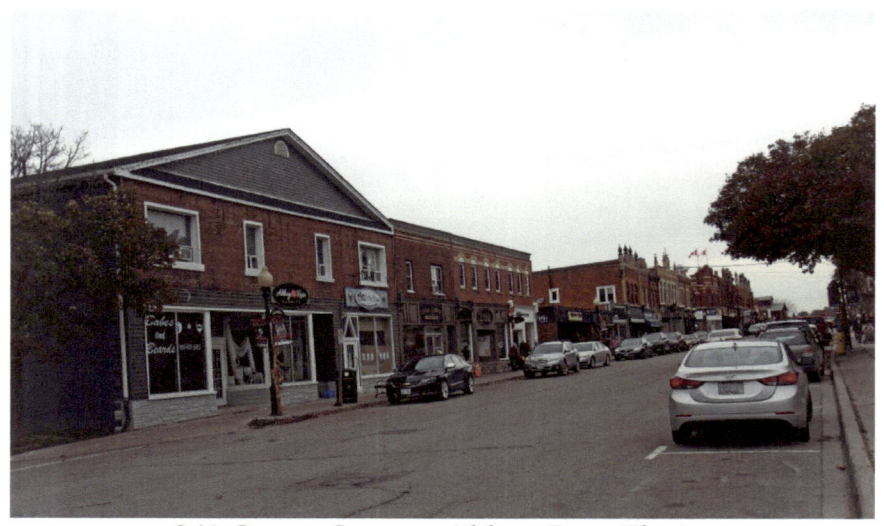

261 Queen Street – Abbey Rose Florist

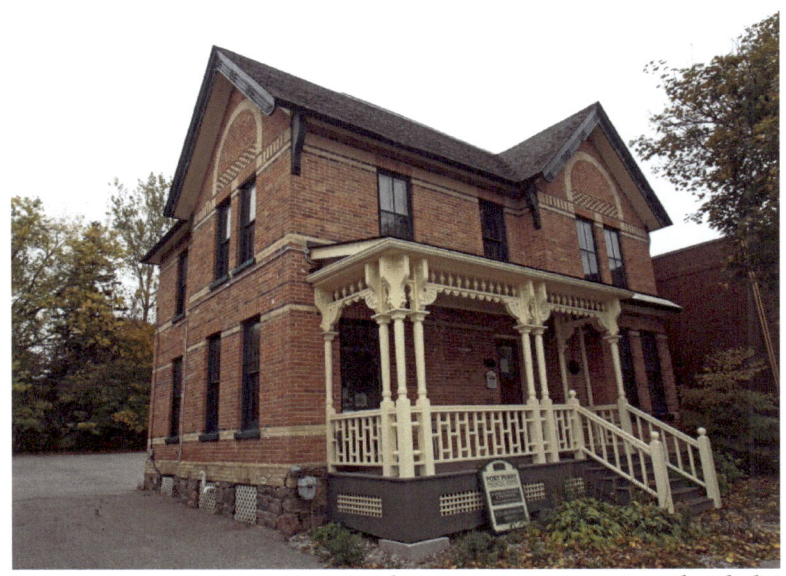

250 Queen Street – Dr. Orr Graham, a veterinarian, had this house built in 1886. Upon his retirement in 1909, he sold his house and practice to Dr. John T. Elliot. Dr. Coates arrived in 1910. In 2010, Michael and Frank Konopaski purchased the property and operate their business Scugog Financial and Scugog Accounting Professional Corporation.

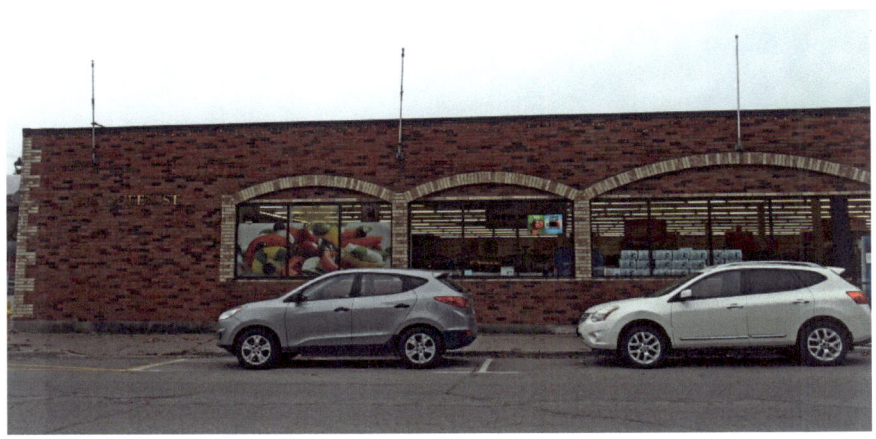

278 Queen Street

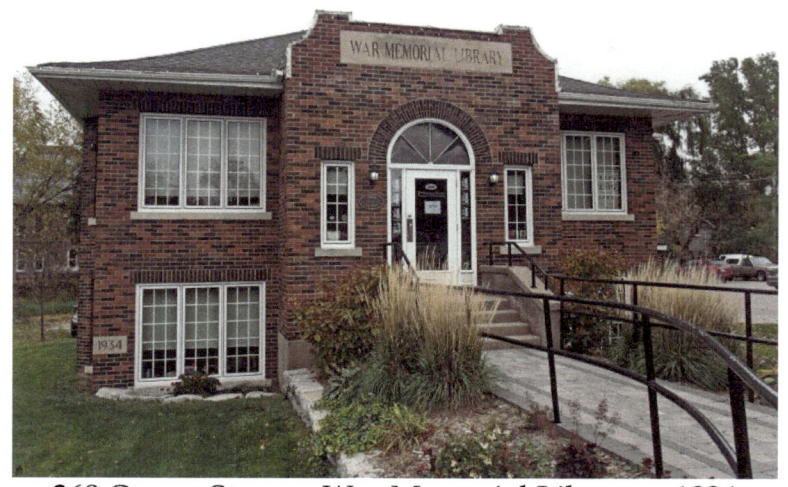

269 Queen Street – War Memorial Library – 1934

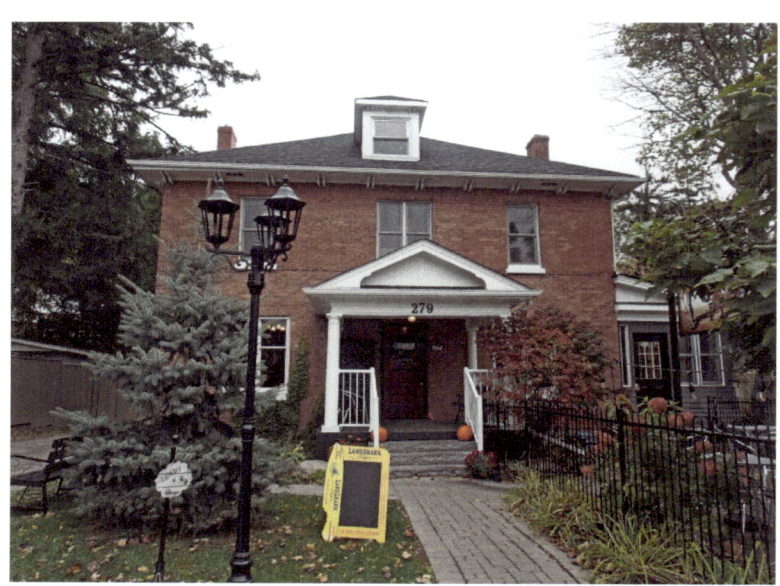

279 Queen Street – dormer in attic, pediment above door

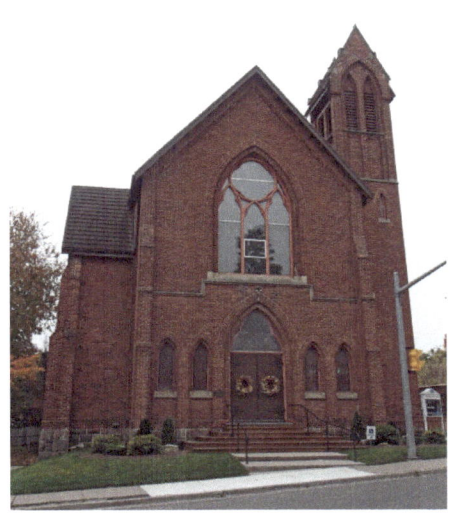

294 Queen Street – Port Perry United Church (1886 – Port Perry Methodist Church) – two storys plus tower, red brick with Ohio cut stone dressings, stained glass window

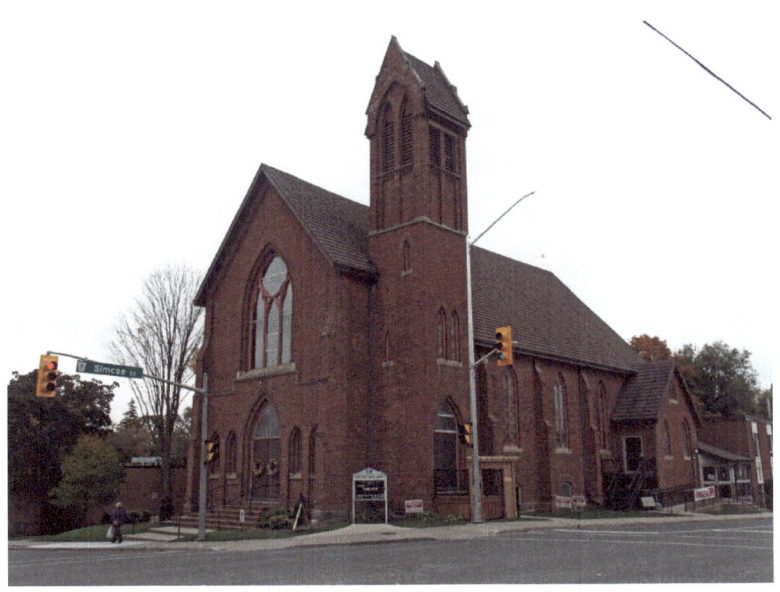

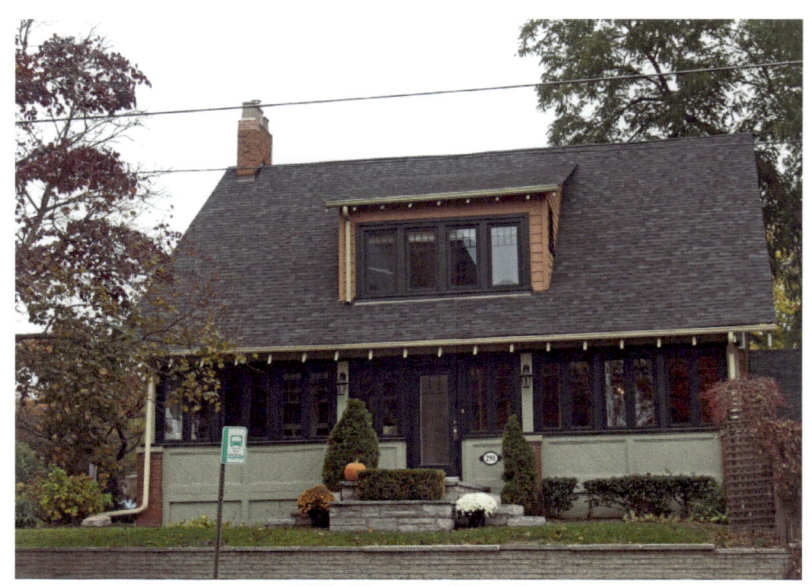

291 Queen Street

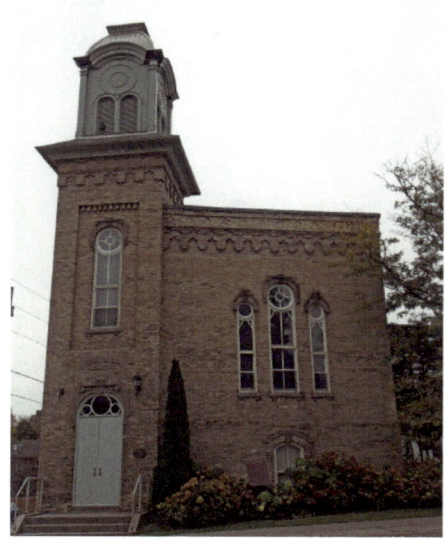

302 Queen Street – Former Port Perry Town Hall – Constructed in 1873, first project of Joseph Bigelow, the first Reeve of Port Perry. Many architectural features of Italianate style, reproduction of the original bell tower.

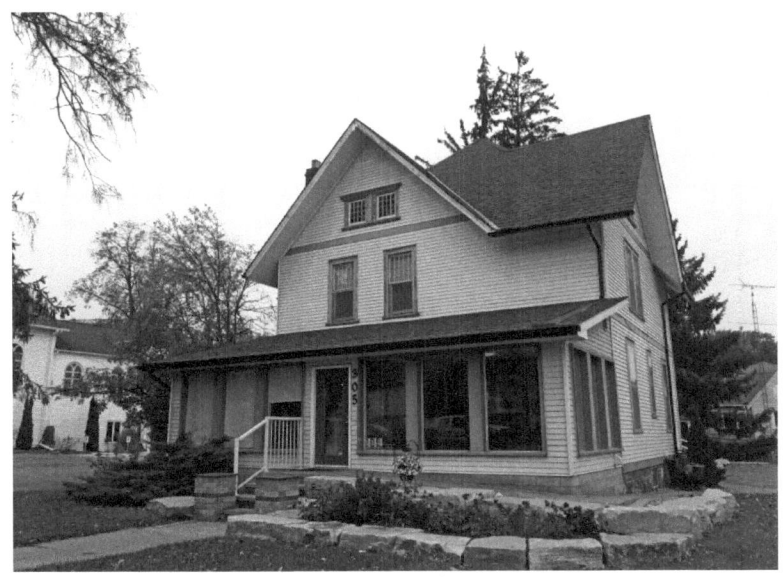

305 Queen Street

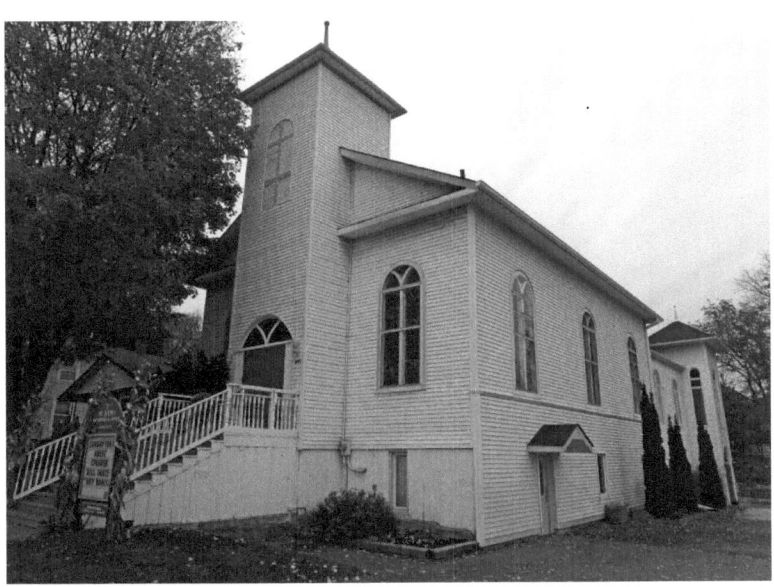

319 Queen Street – St. John's Presbyterian Church – two story plus tower, wood siding – c. 1870

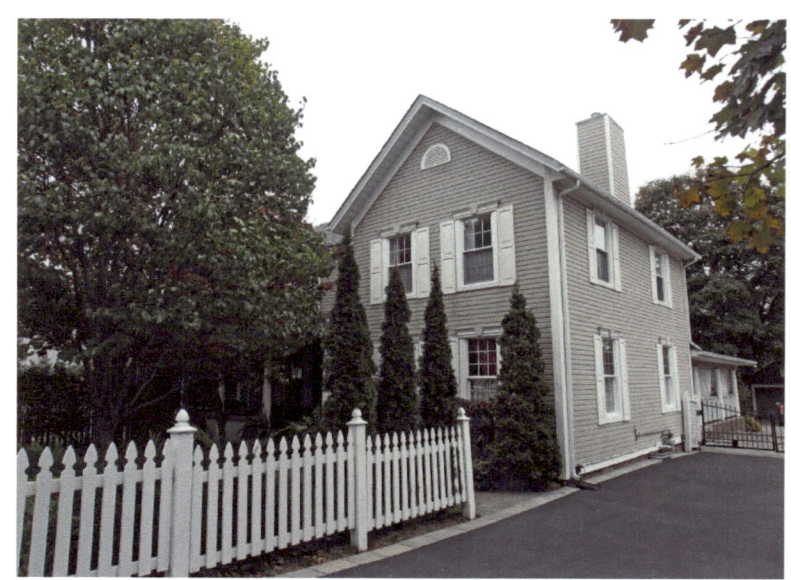

324 Queen Street – William T. Parrish House – 2 story, aluminum siding, c. 1874

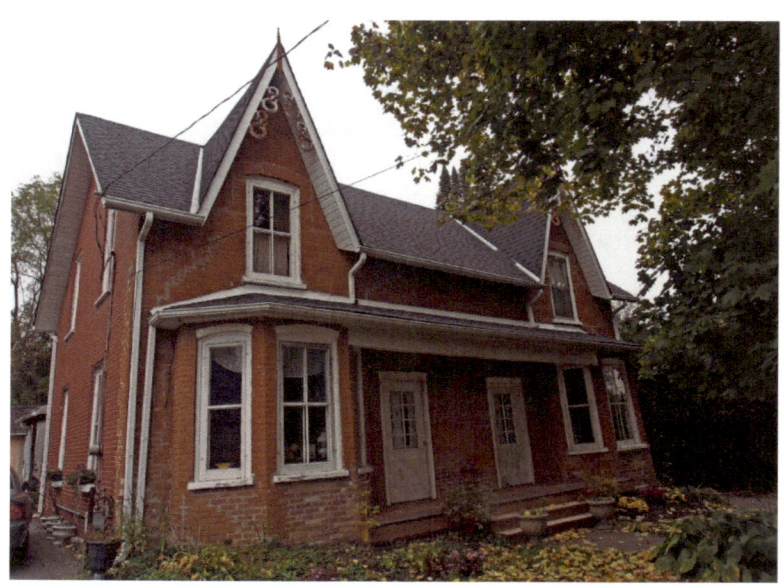

Queen Street – Gothic – c. 1890

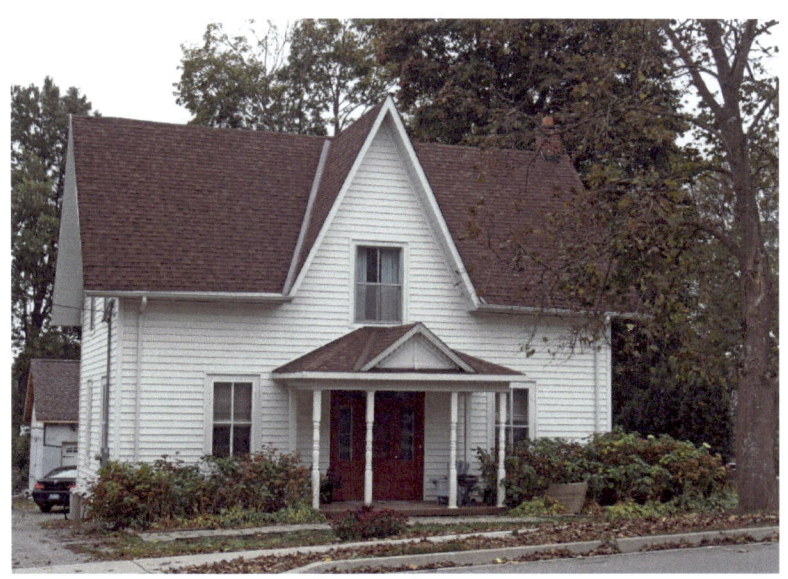

Queen Street

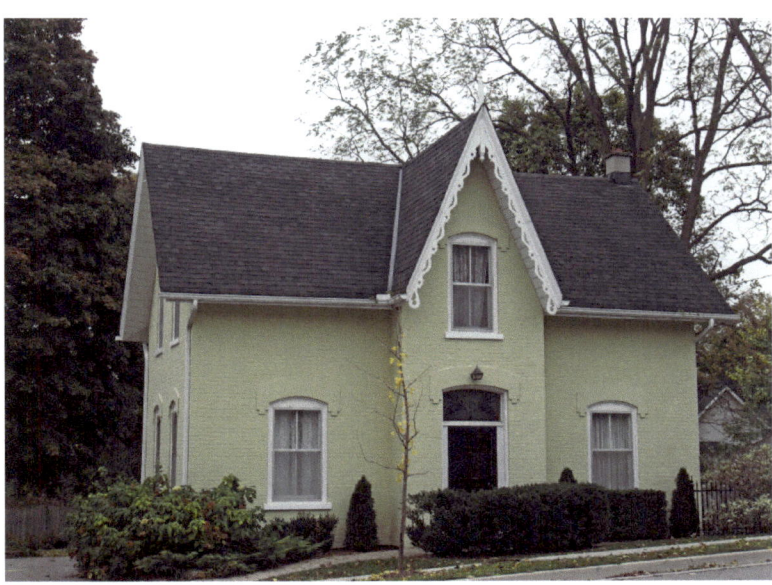

Queen Street – Gothic Revival - verge board trim and finial on gable

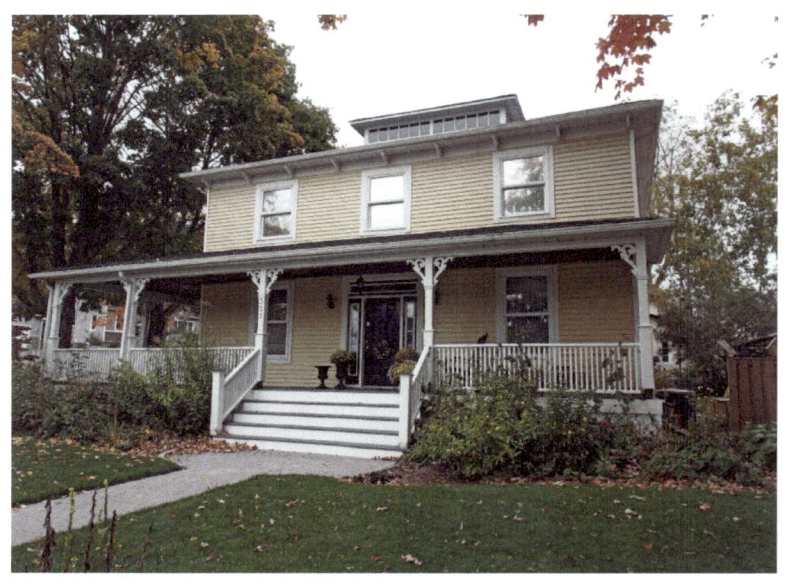

327 Queen Street – Dr. Richard Jones' residence – two story, aluminum siding, belvedere on rooftop – c. 1897

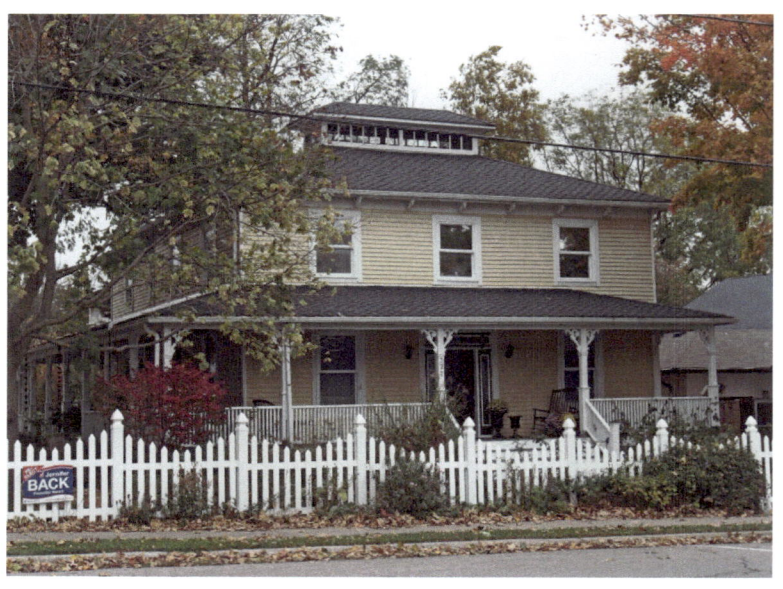

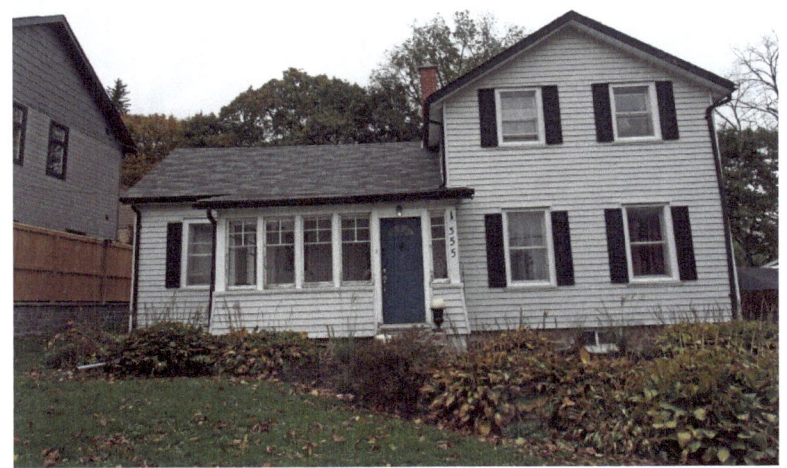

395 Queen Street

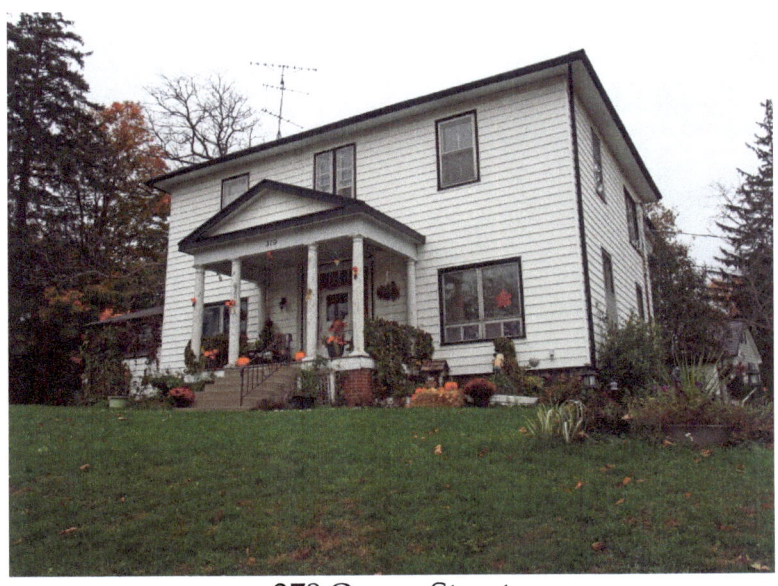

379 Queen Street

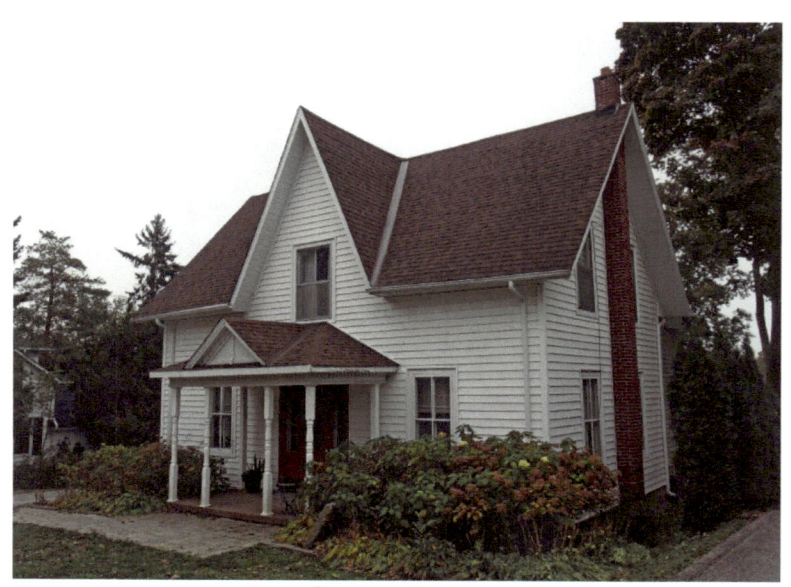

Queen Street

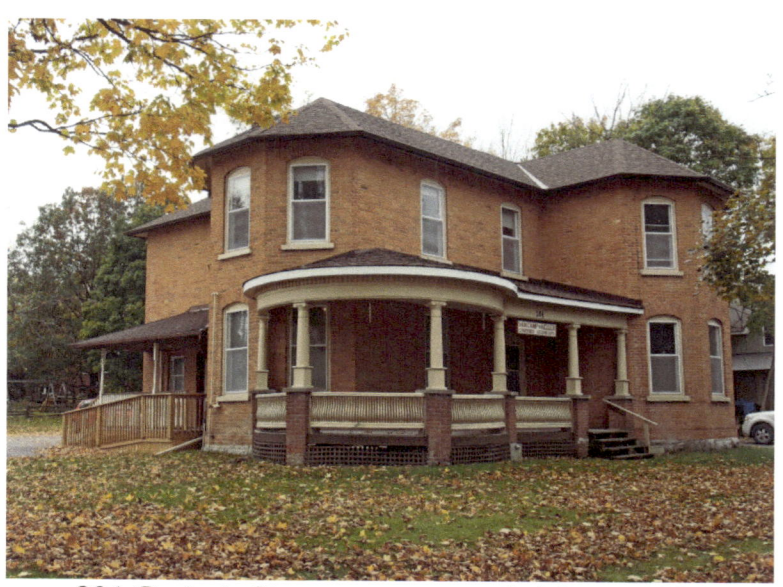

204 Casimir Street – two story brick – c. 1885

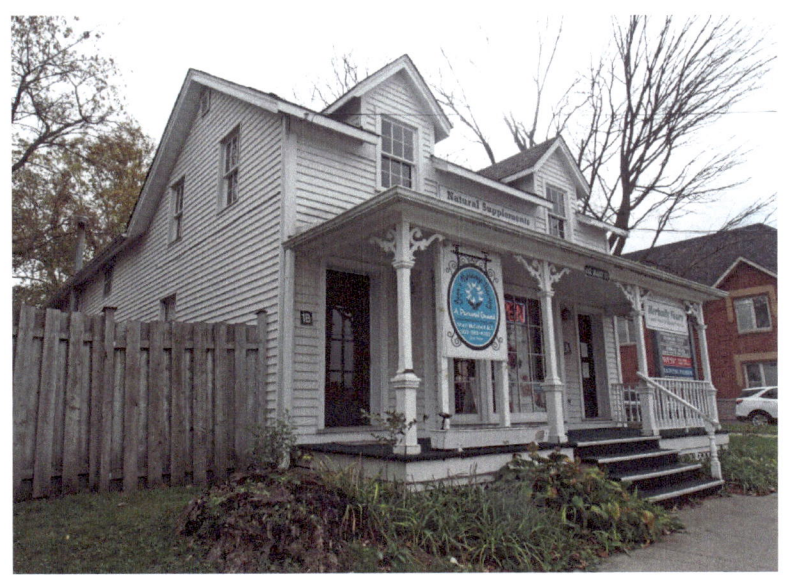

180 Mary Street

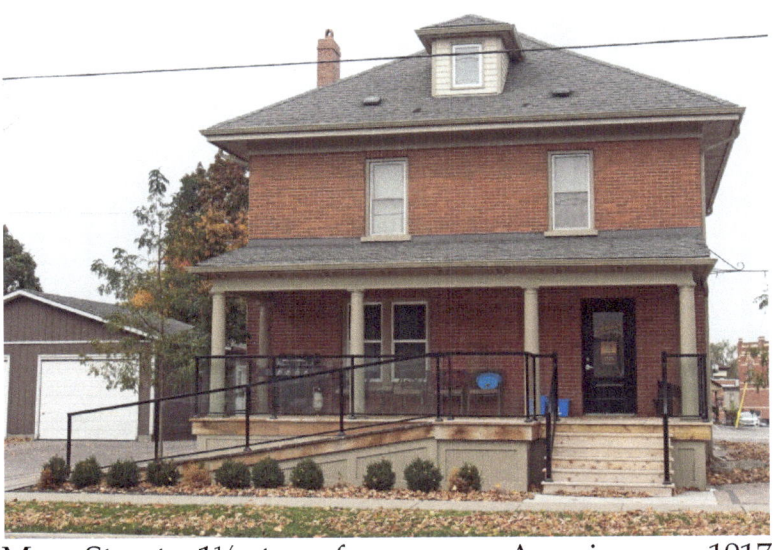

209 Mary Street – 1½ story, four-square American – c. 1917 – dormer in hipped roof

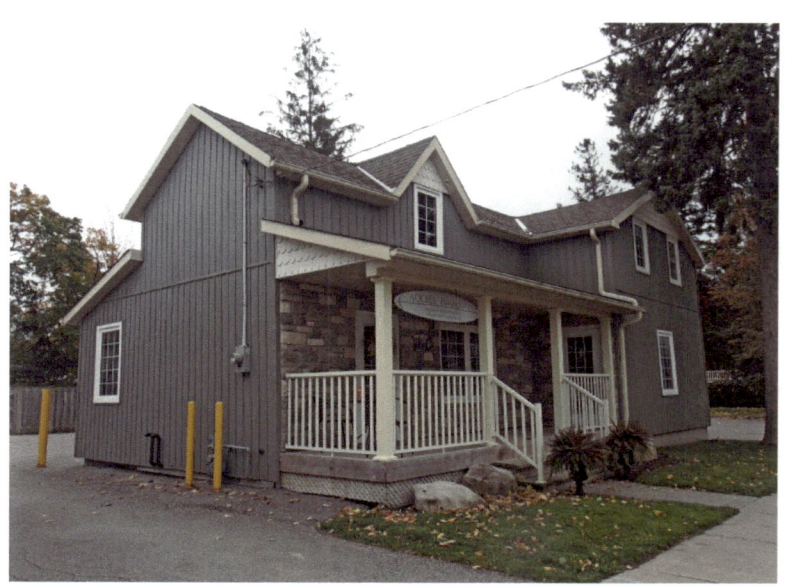

214 Mary Street – the childhood home of Daniel David Palmer – 1½ story L-shaped Victorian – c. 1870

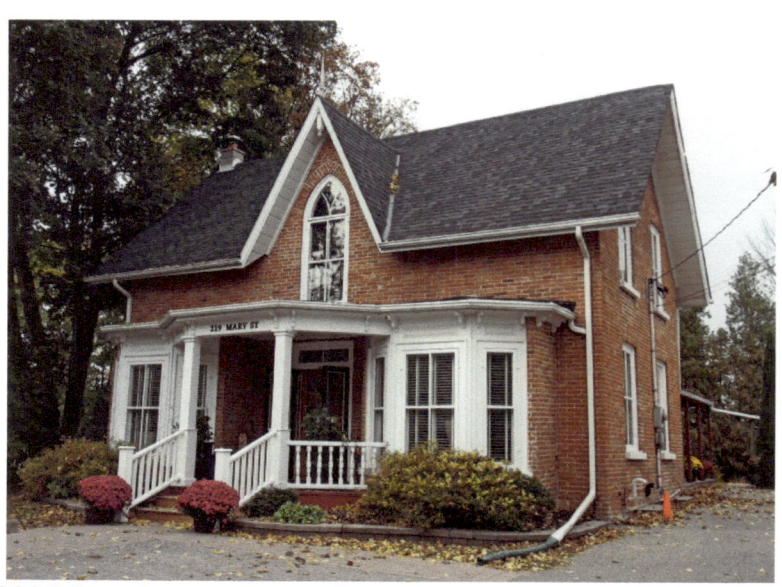

229 Mary Street – S.E. Allen Residence – 1½ story, brick, Victorian Gothic, symmetrical centre hall plan, c. 1870

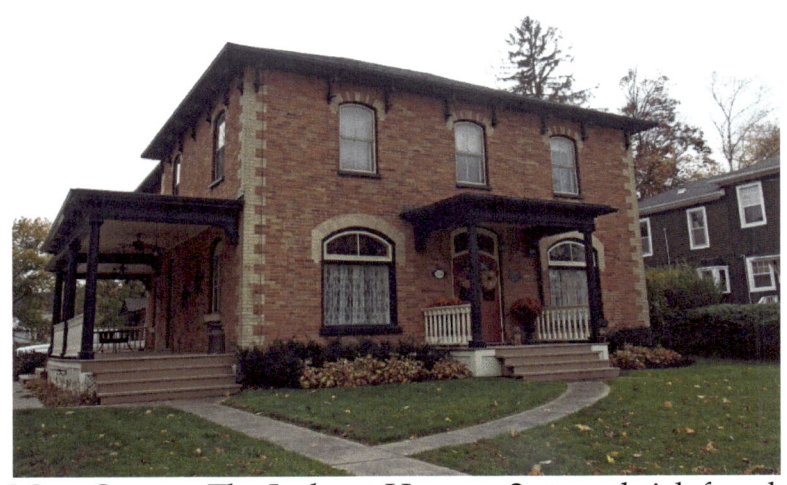

234 Mary Street – The Jackson House – 2 story, brick façade, c. 1880 – cornice brackets, corner quoins

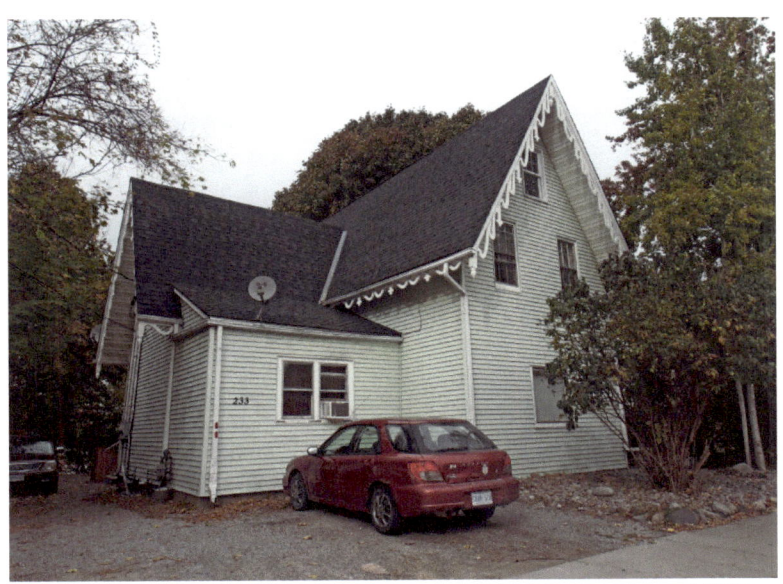

233 Mary Street – 1½ story, Gothic Revival, c. 1870

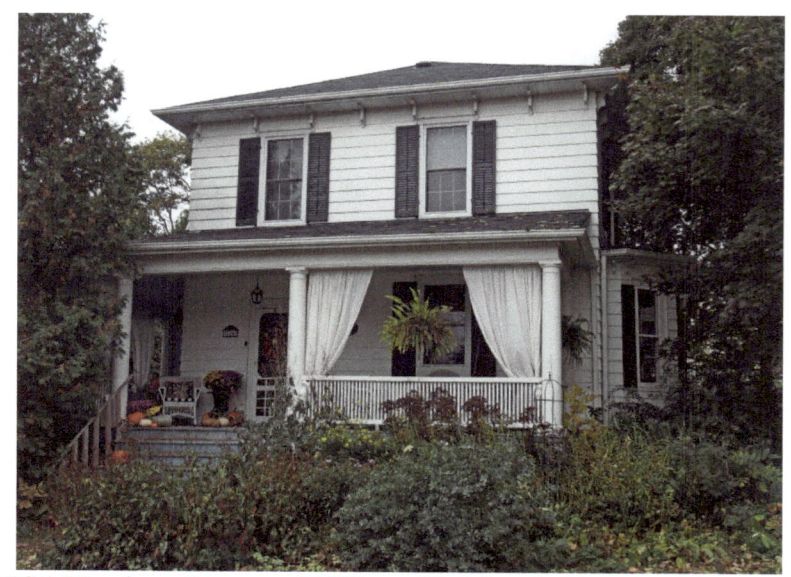

126 Bigelow Street – William H. Marsh, Baptist Minister – c. 1873

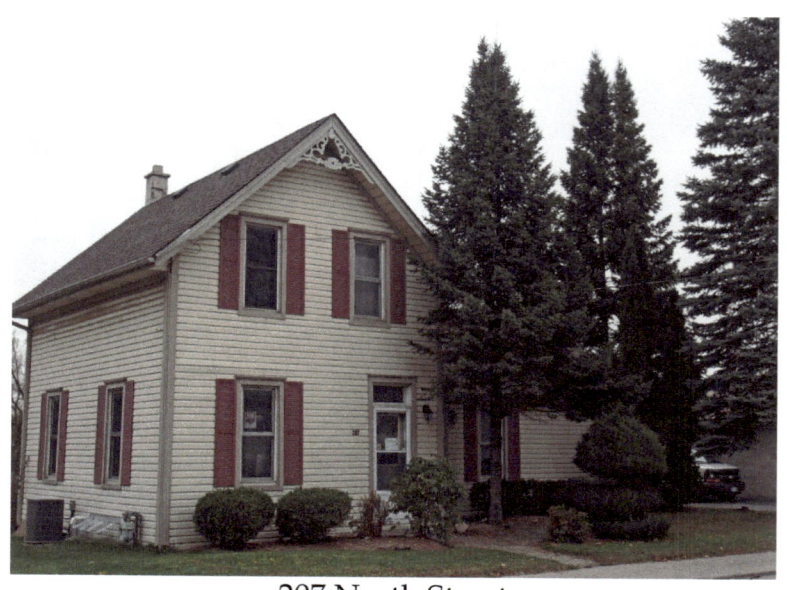

207 North Street

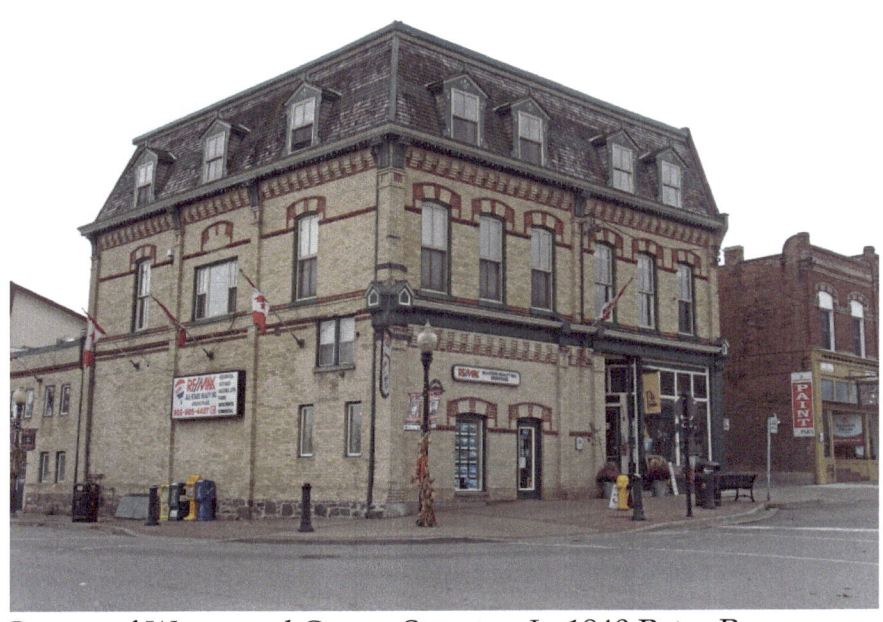

Corner of Water and Queen Streets – In 1840 Peter Perry purchased forty acres in downtown Port Perry and in 1844 he built a frame building which house a store, trading post, and a home for his agent, Chester Draper. Immediately after Perry's death is 1851, the property was bought by Mason and Phillips who turned it into a hotel. Henry Charles purchased it in 1867. The present yellow building was built after the fire of 1884. The hotel had thirty rooms including a dining room and at the street level were two stores including a sample room where salesmen could display their wares. They named it the St. Charles Hotel after Henry Charles.

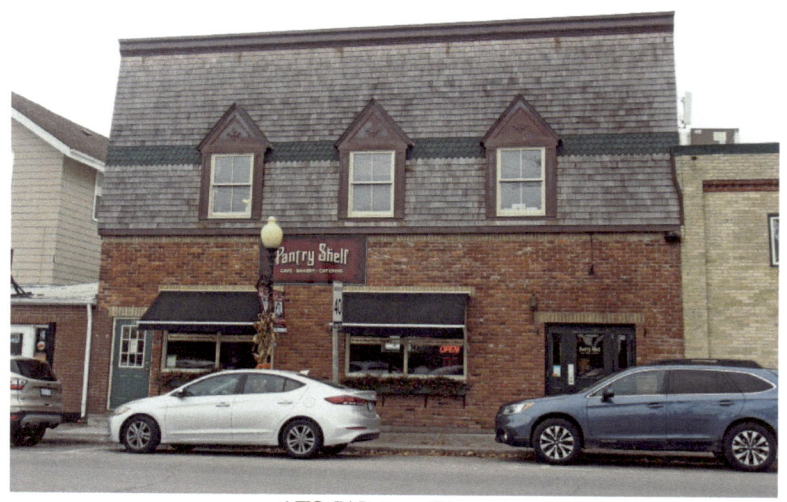

172 Water Street

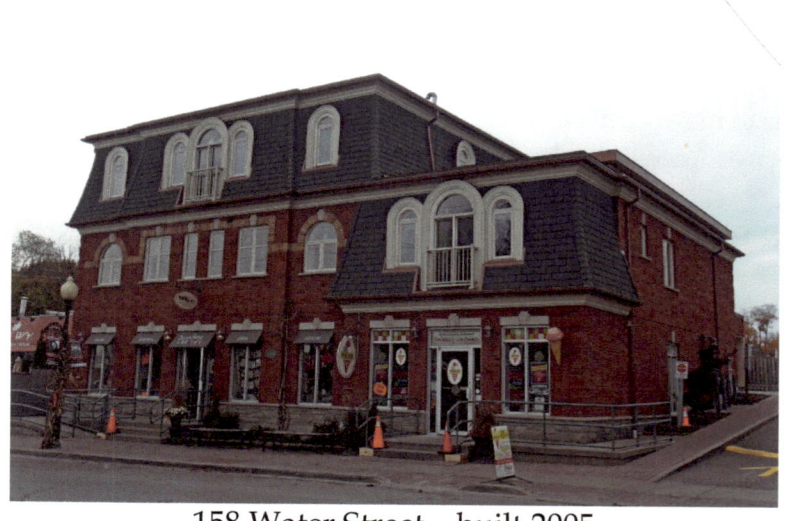

158 Water Street – built 2005

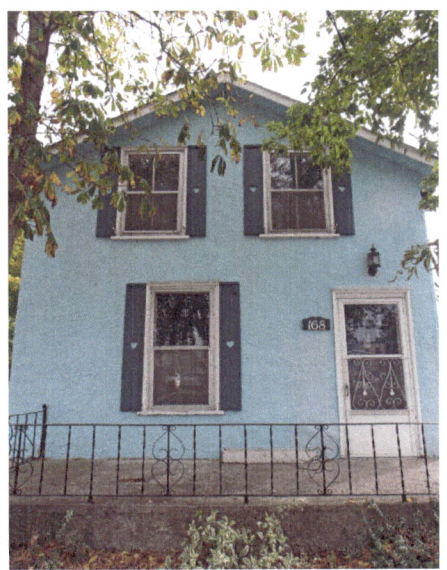

168 Water Street

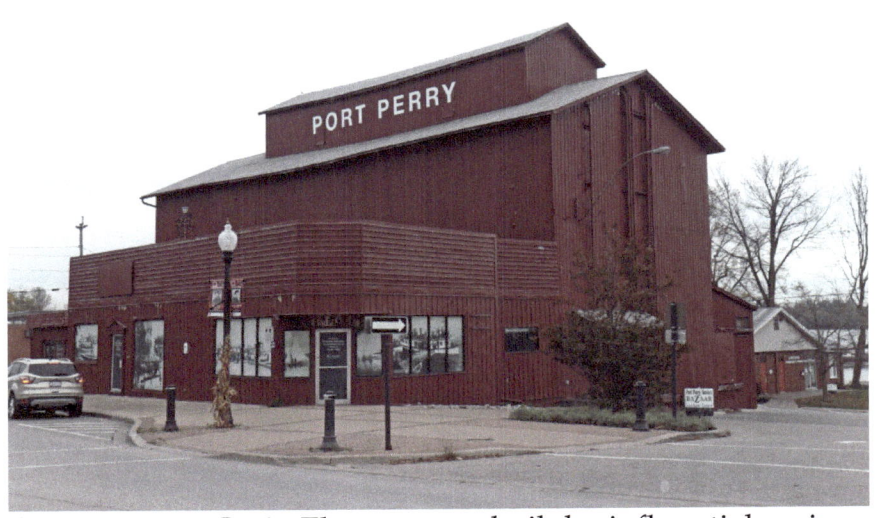

The Port Perry Grain Elevator was built by influential grain merchant George Currie in 1874 on the waterfront at the foot of Queen Street. It is 71 feet high and was used for grain storage. It operated as a mill until its closing in 1979.

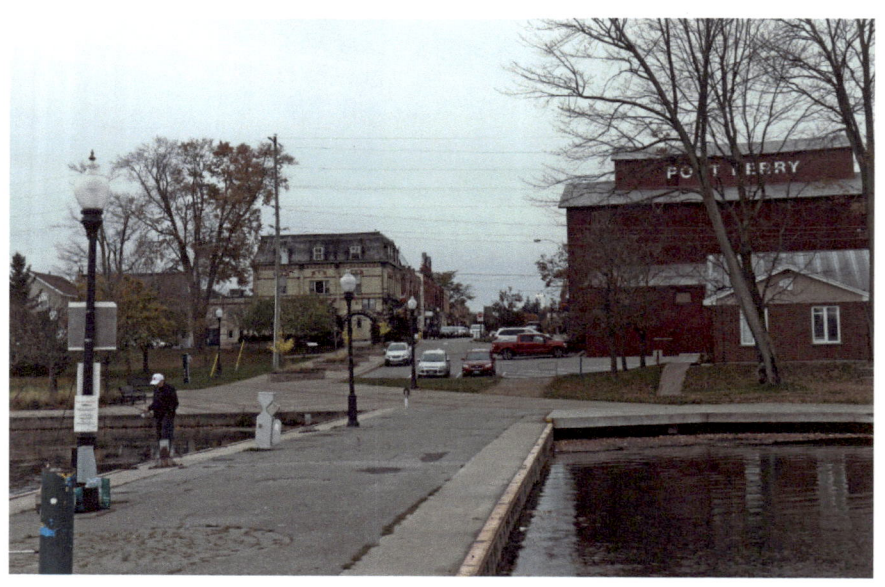

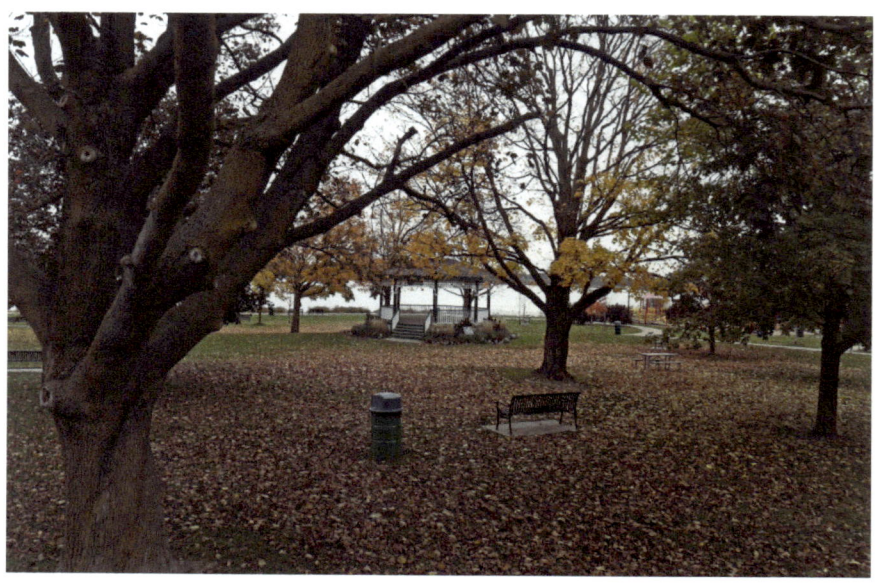

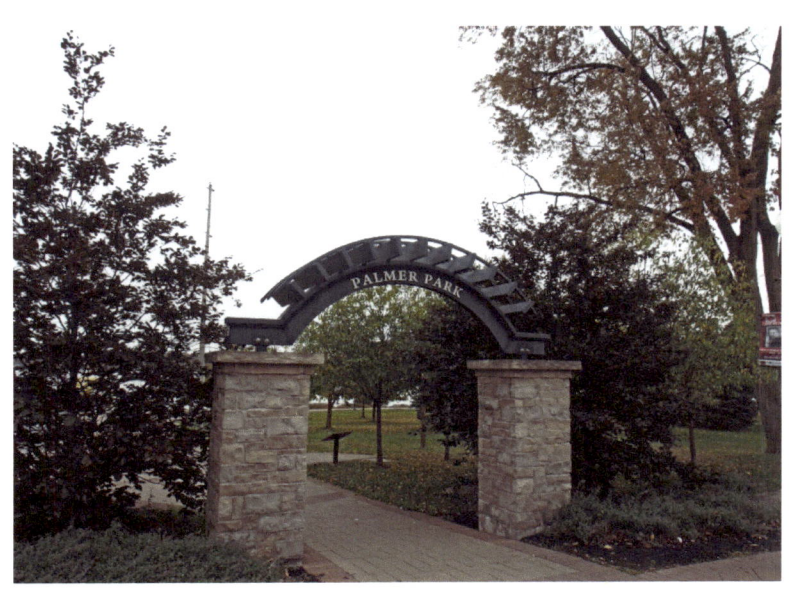

175 Water Street - Palmer Park archway

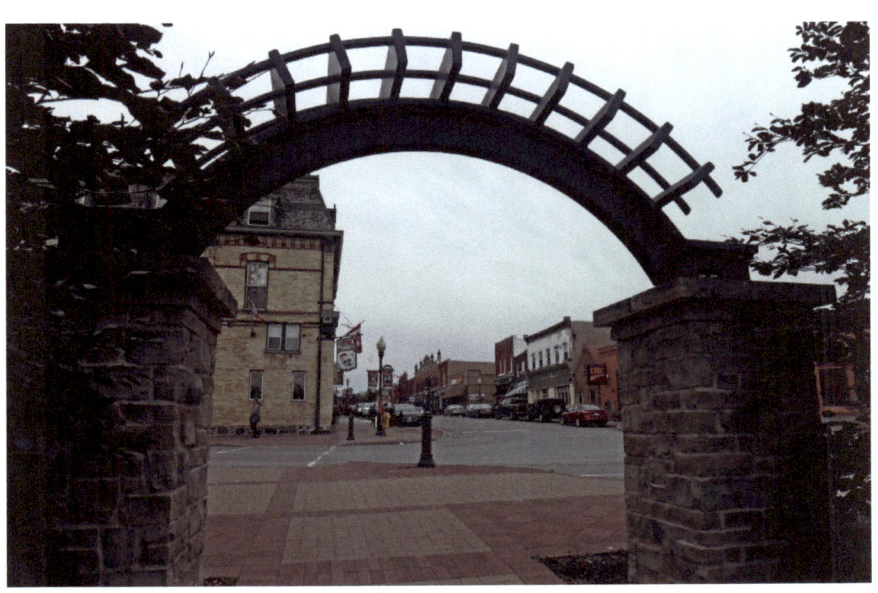

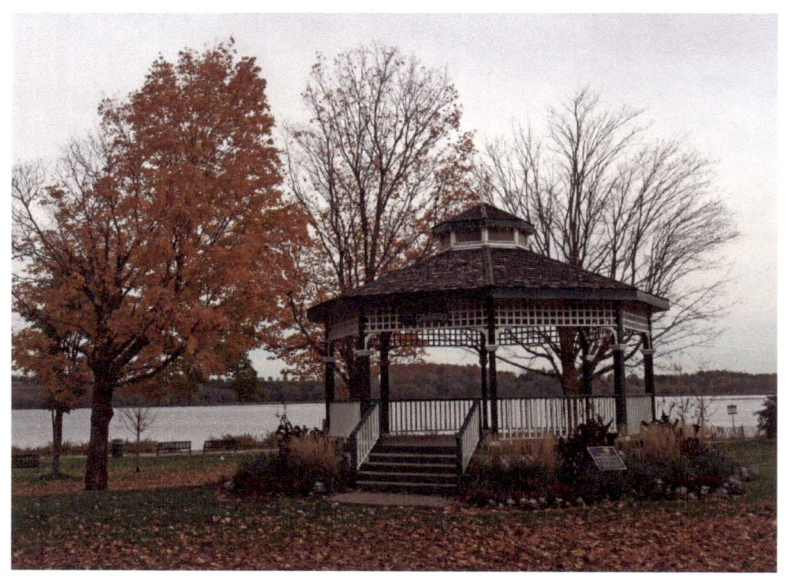

Looking out on Lake Scugog which is 23.55 kilometers long, 5.8 kilometers at its widest, and has a shoreline of 172 kilometers.

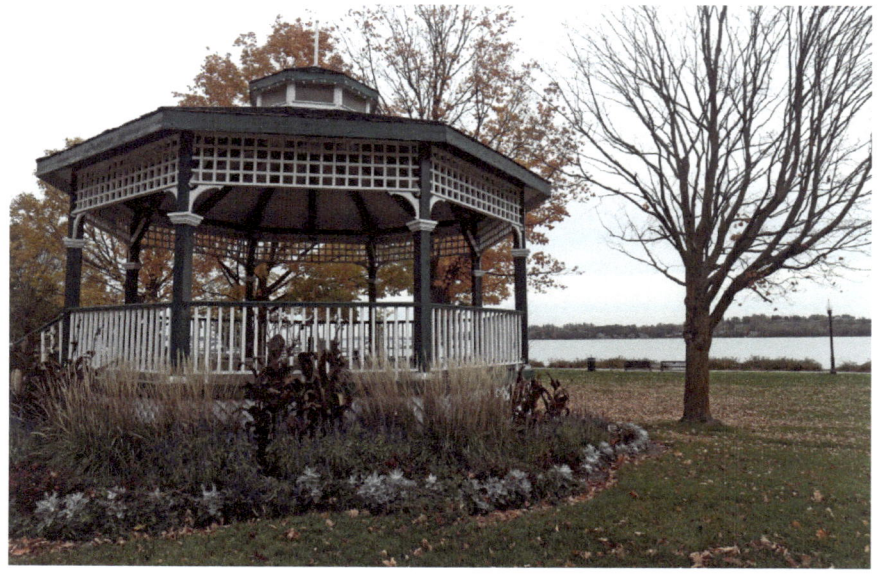

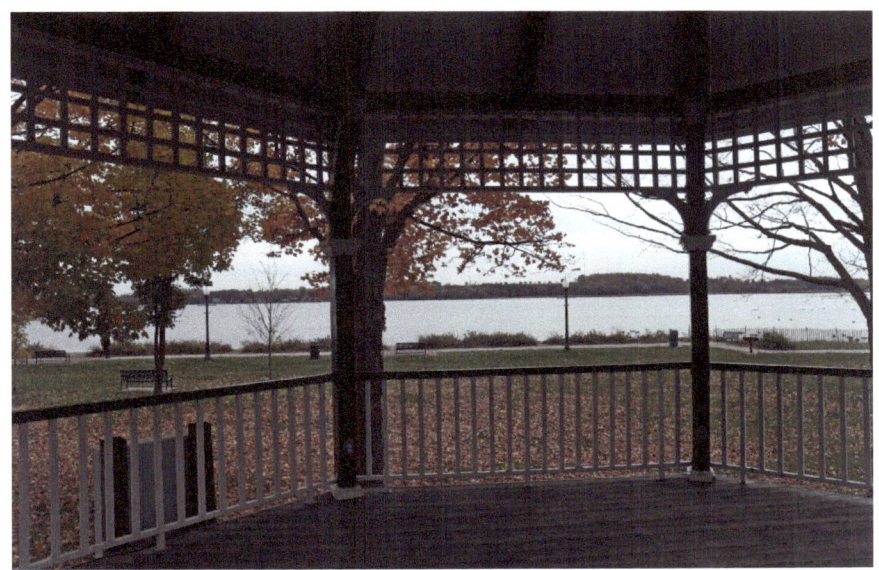

Lake Scugog was created in 1829 after a dam was built across the Scugog River at Lindsay which caused the water to rise in the Lake Scugog basin between six and eight feet. Lake Scugog is part of the Kawartha Lakes water system. It flows north to the Scugog River which feeds Sturgeon River and the rest of the Trent-Severn Waterway.

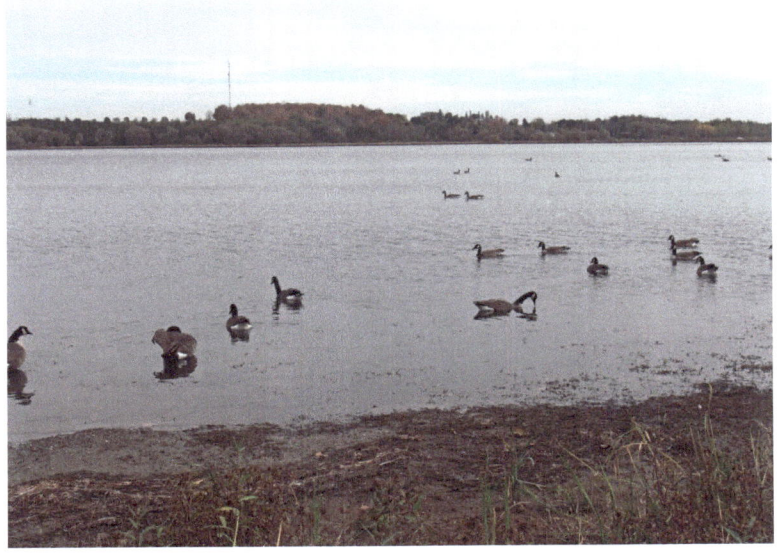

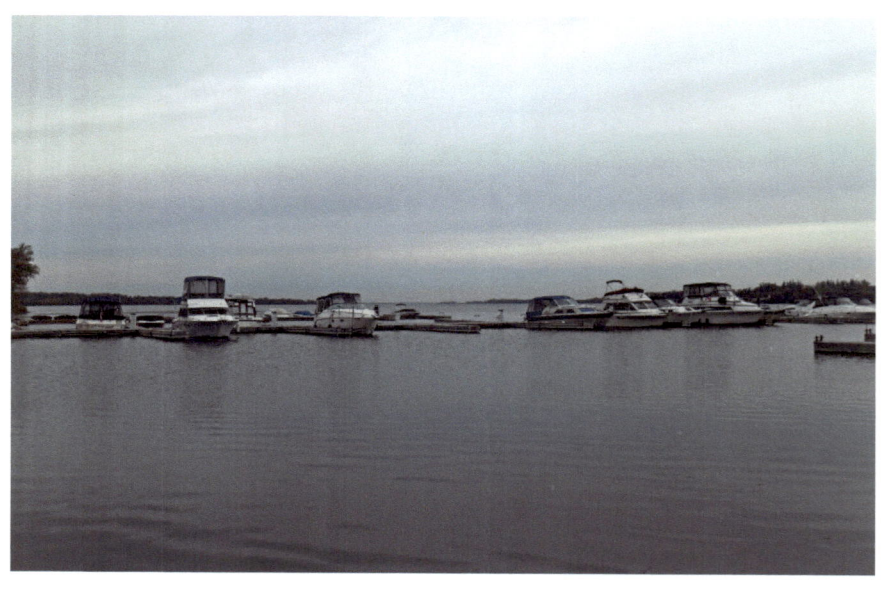

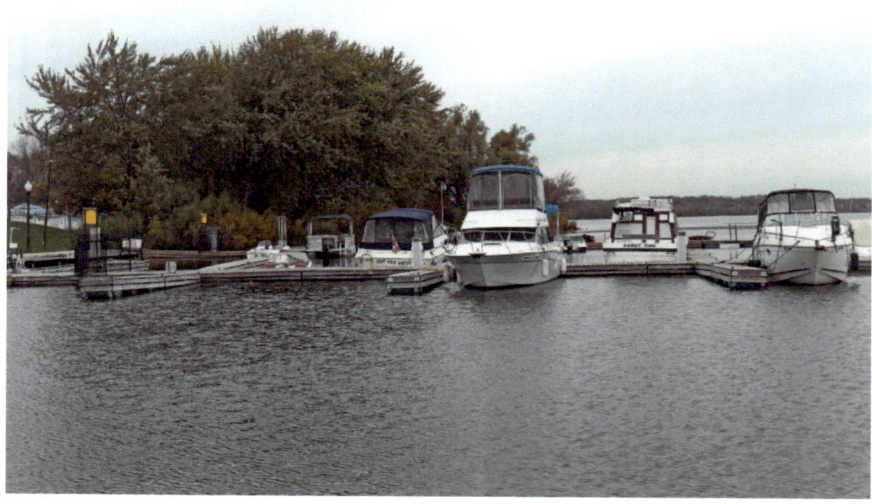

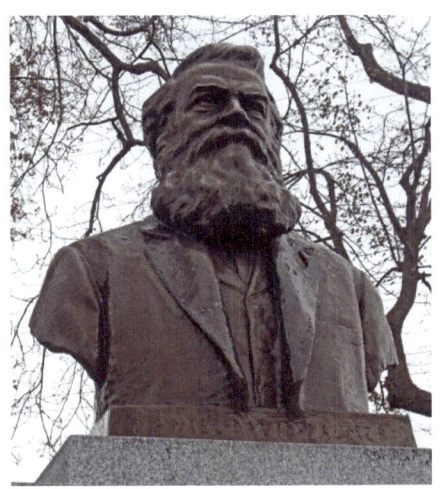 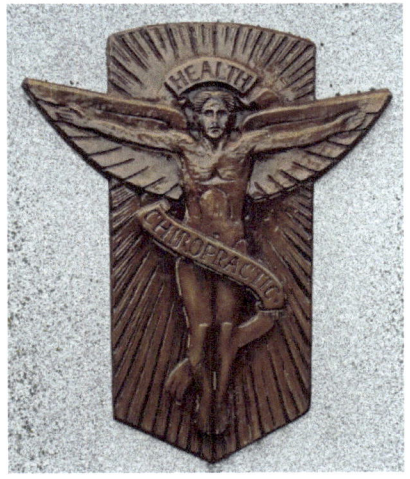

Daniel David Palmer (1845-1913) was self-educated, well read, and interested in alternative medicine. His clinical observations and analyses led him to conclude that proper spinal alignment could restore nerve flow and ensure good general health. He published books on chiropractic treatment and founded and taught at several chiropractic schools. He is recognized as the founder of chiropractic.

Epsom

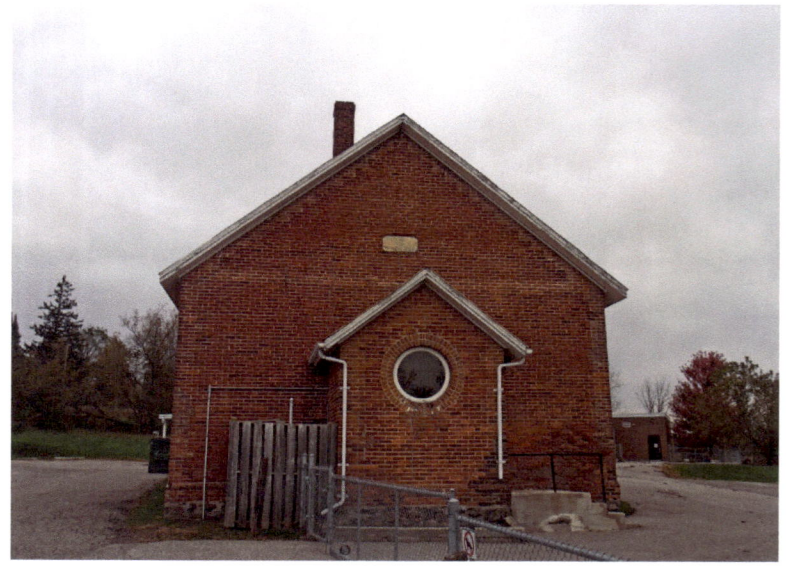

Epsom Public School – S.S. No. 11 – erected A.D. 1836

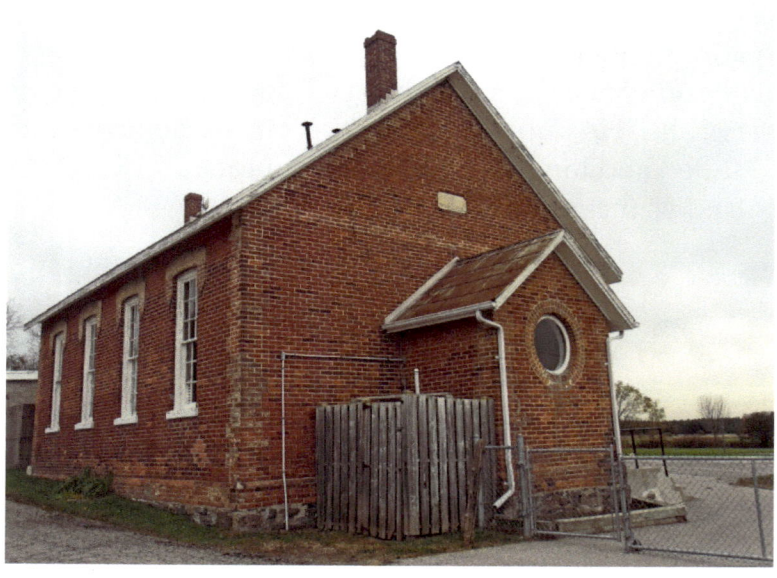

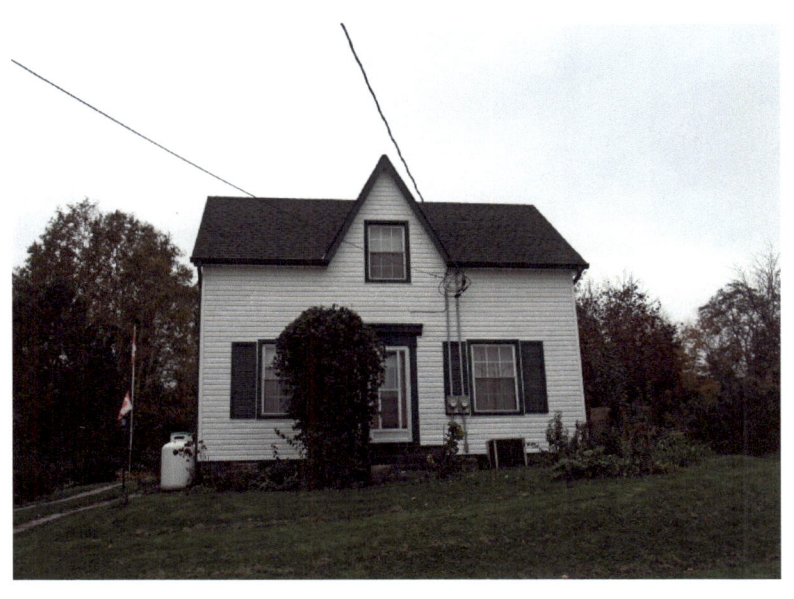

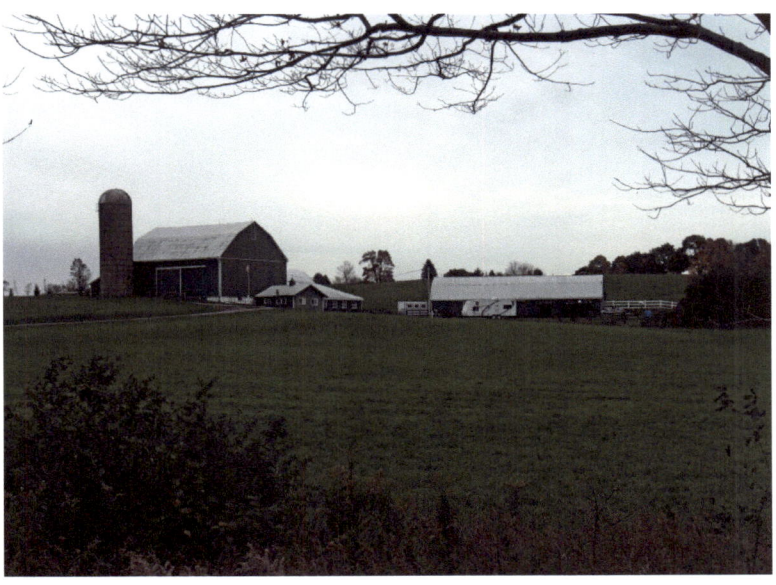

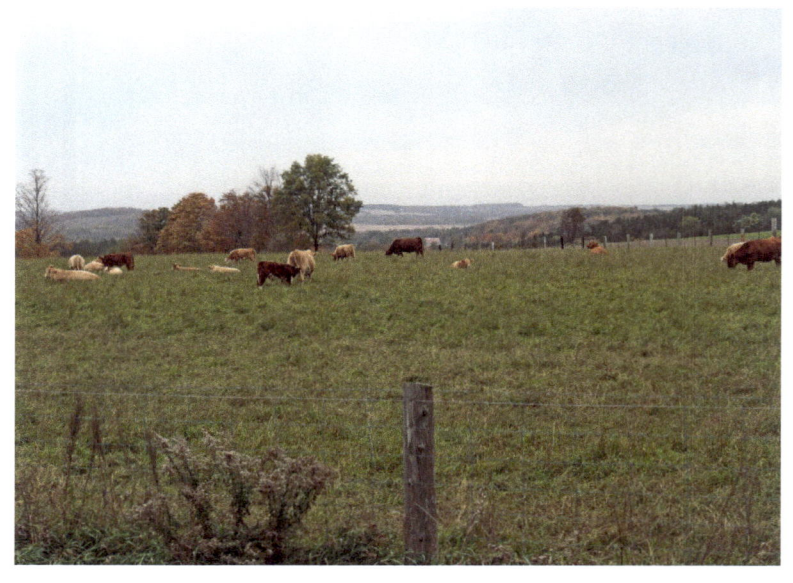

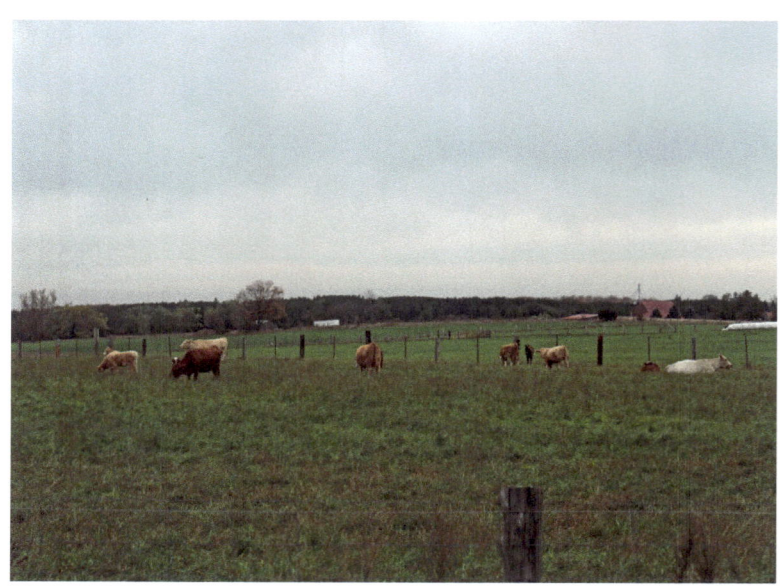

Building Styles

The **American Four Square** is a house style popular from the mid-1890s to the late 1930s. A reaction to the ornate and mass-produced elements of the Victorian and other Revival styles popular throughout the last half of the 19th century, the American Foursquare was plain, often incorporating handcrafted woodwork. This style incorporates elements of the Prairie School and the Craftsman styles. It is also sometimes called Transitional Period. The hallmarks of the style include a basically square, boxy design, two-and-one-half stories high, usually with four large, boxy rooms to a floor, a center dormer, and a large front porch with wide stairs. The boxy shape provides a maximum amount of interior room space, to use a small city lot to best advantage. Other common features included a hipped roof, arched entries between common rooms, built-in cabinetry, and Craftsman-style woodwork.

The **Craftsman** home style incorporates natural elements and simple detailing to create a home with a relaxed and informal appeal. At its height of popularity in the early 20th century, the Craftsman style of home was mostly applied to small, affordable bungalows. In recent years, however, the quality and architectural details of the Craftsman style has reemerged and been found to translate well onto just about any building design. Craftsman architectural details are modest yet meaningful. Its use of natural and local building materials can be among the least expensive to buy and work with. Materials used may be stucco, wood, brick, stone, cedar shakes (shingles), and lap siding. Usually, you will see a combination of two or three of the materials blended in perfect harmony in the craftsman house design. Unifying elements include a low-pitched roof, extended eave overhang with exposed rafter tails, the use of brackets at gables, windows with divided panes in the upper sash and a single pane in the lower sash, medium to large front porches with heavy, square or tapered columns that may be full length or resting on a base that is dressed with stone or stucco.

Gothic Revival, 1830-1890 – These decorative buildings have sharply-pitched gables with highly detailed verge boards, pointed-arch window openings, and dichromatic brickwork. It is a common style in Ontario.

Italianate, 1850-1900 – A two story rectangular building with a mild hip roof, a projecting frontispiece, and generous eaves with ornate cornice brackets was the basis of the style; often there are large sash windows, quoins, ornate detailing on the windows, belvederes and wraparound verandahs. Italianate commercial buildings often have cast iron cresting and elegant window surrounds.

Prairie style, 1900-1940 - is one of the only purely North American styles. The horizontal lines, projecting eaves and geometric patterning of finishes and windows contrast sharply with the more formal, Classical styles taken from ancient Greece. Vernacular materials, stone, brick, and natural wood were preferred for finishes and often stained glass with patterns taken from nature was added. Prairie buildings are generally domestic and have a geometric patterning that is immediately evident. The complete lack of historicizing detail is deliberate and points to the trends found later in the century.

Second Empire, 1860-1880 – The mansard roof is the most noteworthy feature of this style and is evidence of the French origins. Projecting central towers and one or two-story bays can also be present.

Victorian - In Ontario, a Victorian style building can be seen as any building built between 1840 and 1900 that doesn't fit into any of the other categories. It encompasses a large group of buildings constructed in brick, stone, and timber, using an eclectic mixture of Classical and Gothic motifs.

Other Books by Barbara Raue

Coins of Gold
Arrows, Indians and Love
The Life and Times of Barbara
The Cromwell Family Book
Laura Secord Discovered
Daddy Where Are You?

Montana Series
Book 1: Montana Dream
Book 2: Life on the Montana Frontier
Book 3: Montana to Boston and Back
Book 4: Montana Sons Go to War
Book 5: Montana Sons Return from War

Donaldson Series
Book 1: Rite of Passage
Book 2: Rite of Marriage

© 2022 by Barbara Raue - All the photos in this book have been taken with my cameras. I own the rights to them.

Barbara is The Authority on Saving Our History One Photo at a Time. She is pursuing her interest in photography and architecture by preserving a record through photos of old buildings from the 1800s and 1900s with their unique architecture. Enjoy the beautiful architecture in the comfort of your living room. Dream about what it was like in those by-gone days. Dream about what it was like to live in a mansion like one of those in this book.

Barbara Raue, a wife, mother and grandmother, is an avid reader and writer. She has researched and compiled several family histories. In 2010, Barbara published her book "Coins of Gold," which celebrates the courageous life of her mother, May Todd. Barbara's second book is a historical fiction "Arrows, Indians and Love" which takes place in Boonesborough, Kentucky during the time of Daniel Boone. In 2013, Barbara published *The Cromwell Family Book* in which she traces her ancestry generations back into Great Britain. Her second novel is called *Laura Secord Discovered,* in which the story of Laura's service during the War of 1812 is shared. Barbara's memoir is titled *Daddy Where Are You?* It tells of her life growing up without a father. Five novels in the Montana Series have been published, *Montana Dream, Life on the Montana Frontier, Montana to Boston and Back, Montana Sons Go to War*, and *Montana Sons Return from War*. The Donaldson series of two novels is available: *Rite of Passage* and *Rite of Marriage*.

This is a link to Barbara's website to view all of her books
http://barbararaue.ca

www.ingramcontent.com/pod-product-compliance
Lightning Source LLC
Chambersburg PA
CBHW040242220526
45473CB00001B/335